America in
Prophecy
The begining of the end...

E. G. WHITE

Remnant
Publications

Coldwater MI 49036
www.remnantpublications.com

Copyright © 2008
All Rights Reserved
Printed in the USA

Published by
Remnant Publications
649 East Chicago Road
Coldwater MI 49036
517-279-1304
www.remnantpublications.com

This book is a portion of a work originally published
under the title, *The Great Controversy.*

All Bible Scripture is taken from the King James Version.

Cover design by David Berthiaume
Text design by Greg Solie • AltamontGraphics.com

ISBN 978-1-933291-41-3

Contents

One

—The Pilgrim Fathers—

The English Reformers, while renouncing the doctrines of Romanism, had retained many of its forms. Thus though the authority and the creed of Rome were rejected, not a few of her customs and ceremonies were incorporated into the worship of the Church of England. It was claimed that these things were not matters of conscience; that though they were not commanded in Scripture, and hence were nonessential, yet not being forbidden, they were not intrinsically evil. Their observance tended to narrow the gulf which separated the reformed churches from Rome, and it was urged that they would promote the acceptance of the Protestant faith by Romanists.

To the conservative and compromising, these arguments seemed conclusive. But there was another class that did not so judge. The fact that these customs "tended to bridge over the chasm between Rome and the Reformation" (Martyn, volume 5, page 22), was in their view a conclusive argument against retaining them. They looked upon them as badges of the slavery from which they had been delivered and to which they had no disposition to return. They reasoned that God has in His word established the regulations governing His worship, and that men are not at liberty to add to these or to detract from them. The very beginning of the great apostasy was in seeking to supplement the authority of God by that of the church. Rome began by enjoining what God had not forbidden, and she ended by forbidding what He had explicitly enjoined.

Many earnestly desired to return to the purity and simplicity which characterized the primitive church. They regarded many of the established customs of the English Church as monuments of idolatry, and they could not in conscience unite in her worship. But the church, being supported by the civil authority, would permit no dissent from her forms. Attendance upon her service was required by law, and unauthorized assemblies for religious worship were prohibited, under penalty of imprisonment, exile, and death.

At the opening of the seventeenth century the monarch who had just ascended the throne of England declared his determination to make the Puritans "conform, or ... harry them out of the land, or else worse." George Bancroft, *History of the United States of America*, pt. 1, ch. 12, par. 6. Hunted, persecuted, and imprisoned, they could discern in the future no promise of better days, and many yielded to the conviction that for such as would serve God according to the dictates of their conscience, "England was ceasing forever to be a habitable place."—J. G. Palfrey, *History of New England*, ch. 3, par. 43. Some at last determined to seek refuge in Holland. Difficulties, losses, and imprisonment were encountered. Their purposes were thwarted, and they were betrayed into the hands of their enemies. But steadfast perseverance finally conquered, and they found shelter on the friendly shores of the Dutch Republic.

In their flight they had left their houses, their goods, and their means of livelihood. They were strangers in a strange land, among a people of different language and customs. They were forced to resort to new and untried occupations to earn their bread. Middle-aged men, who had spent their lives in tilling the soil, had now to learn mechanical trades. But they cheerfully accepted the situation and lost no time in idleness or repining. Though often pinched with poverty, they thanked God for the blessings which were still granted them and found their joy in unmolested spiritual communion. "They knew they were pilgrims, and looked not much on those things, but lifted up their eyes to heaven, their dearest country, and quieted their spirits."—Bancroft, pt. 1, ch. 12, par. 15.

In the midst of exile and hardship their love and faith waxed strong. They trusted the Lord's promises, and He did not fail them in time of need. His angels were by their side, to encourage and support them. And when God's hand seemed pointing them across the sea, to a land where they might found for themselves a state, and leave to their children the precious heritage of religious liberty, they went forward, without shrinking, in the path of providence.

God had permitted trials to come upon His people to prepare them for the accomplishment of His gracious purpose toward them. The church had been brought low, that she might be exalted. God was about to display His power in her behalf, to give to the world another evidence that He will not forsake those who trust in Him. He had overruled events to cause the wrath of Satan and the plots of evil men to advance His glory and to bring His people to a place of security. Persecution and exile were opening the way to freedom.

When first constrained to separate from the English Church, the Puritans had joined themselves together by a solemn covenant, as the Lord's free people, "to walk together in all His ways made known or to be made known to them."—J. Brown, *The Pilgrim Fathers*, page 74. Here was the true spirit of reform, the vital principle of Protestantism. It was with this purpose that the Pilgrims departed from Holland to find a home in the New World. John Robinson, their pastor, who was providentially prevented from accompanying them, in his farewell address to the exiles said:

"Brethren, we are now erelong to part asunder, and the Lord knoweth whether I shall live ever to see your faces more. But whether the Lord hath appointed it or not, I charge you before God and His blessed angels to follow me no farther than I have followed Christ. If God should reveal anything to you by any other instrument of His, be as ready to receive it as ever you were to receive any truth of my ministry; for I am very confident the Lord hath more truth and light yet to break forth out of His holy word."—Martyn, vol. 5, p. 70.

"For my part, I cannot sufficiently bewail the condition of the reformed churches, who are come to a period in religion, and will go at present no farther than the instruments of their reformation. The Lutherans cannot be drawn to go beyond what Luther saw; ... and the Calvinists, you see, stick fast where they were left by that great man of God, who yet saw not all things. This is a misery much to be lamented; for though they were burning and shining lights in their time, yet they penetrated not into the whole counsel of God, but were they now living, would be as willing to embrace further light as that which they first received."—D. Neal, *History of the Puritans*, vol. 1, p. 269.

"Remember your church covenant, in which you have agreed to walk in all the ways of the Lord, made or to be made known unto you. Remember your promise and covenant with God and with one another, to receive whatever light and truth shall be made known to you from His written word; but withal, take heed, I beseech you, what you receive for truth, and compare it and weigh it with other scriptures of truth before you accept it; for it is not possible the Christian world should come so lately out of such thick antichristian darkness, and that full perfection of knowledge should break forth at once."—Martyn, vol. 5, pp. 70, 71.

It was the desire for liberty of conscience that inspired the Pilgrims to brave the perils of the long journey across the sea, to endure the hardships and dangers of the wilderness, and with God's blessing to lay, on the shores of America, the foundation of a mighty nation. Yet honest and God-fearing as they were, the Pilgrims did not yet comprehend the great principle of religious liberty. The freedom which they sacrificed so much to secure for themselves, they were not equally ready to grant to others. "Very few, even of the foremost thinkers and moralists of the seventeenth century, had any just conception of that grand principle, the outgrowth of the New Testament, which acknowledges God as the sole judge of human faith."—*Ibid.*, vol. 5, p. 297. The doctrine that God has committed to the church the right to control the conscience, and to define and punish heresy, is one of the most deeply rooted of papal errors. While the Reformers rejected the creed of Rome, they were not entirely free from her spirit of intolerance. The dense darkness in which, through the long ages of her rule, popery had enveloped all Christendom, had not even yet been wholly dissipated. Said one of the leading ministers in the colony of Massachusetts Bay: "It was toleration that made the world antichristian; and the church never took harm by the punishment of heretics."—*Ibid.*, vol. 5, p. 335. The regulation was adopted by the colonists that only church members should have a voice in the civil government. A kind of state church was formed, all the people being required to contribute to the support of the clergy, and the magistrates being authorized to suppress heresy. Thus the secular power was in the hands of the church. It was not long before these measures led to the inevitable result—persecution.

Eleven years after the planting of the first colony, Roger Williams came to the New World. Like the early Pilgrims he came to enjoy religious freedom; but, unlike them, he saw—what so few in his time had yet seen—that this freedom was the inalienable right of all, whatever might be their creed. He was an earnest seeker for truth, with Robinson holding it impossible that all the light from God's word had yet been received. Williams "was the first person in modern Christendom to establish civil government on the doctrine of the liberty of conscience, the equality of opinions before the law."—Bancroft, pt. 1, ch. 15, par. 16. He declared it to be the duty of the magistrate to restrain crime, but never to control the conscience. "The public or the magistrates may decide," he said, "what is due from man to man; but when they attempt to prescribe a man's duties to God, they are out of place, and there can be no safety; for it is clear that if the magistrates has the power, he may decree one set of opinions or beliefs today and another tomorrow; as has been done in England by different kings and queens, and by different popes and councils in the Roman Church; so that belief would become a heap of confusion."—Martyn, vol. 5, p. 340.

Attendance at the services of the established church was required under a penalty of fine or imprisonment. "Williams reprobated the law; the worst statute in the English code was that which did but enforce attendance upon the parish church. To compel men to unite with those of a different creed, he regarded as an open violation of their natural rights; to drag to public worship the irreligious and the unwilling, seemed only like requiring hypocrisy. ... 'No one should be bound to worship, or,' he added, 'to maintain a worship, against his own consent.' 'What!' exclaimed his antagonists, amazed at his tenets, 'is not the laborer worthy of his hire?' 'Yes,' replied he, 'from them that hire him.' "—Bancroft, pt. 1, ch. 15, par. 2.

Roger Williams was respected and beloved as a faithful minister, a man of rare gifts, of unbending integrity and true benevolence; yet his steadfast denial of the right of civil magistrates to authority over the church, and his demand for religious liberty, could not be tolerated. The application of this new doctrine, it was urged, would "subvert the fundamental state and government of the country."—*Ibid.,* pt. 1, ch. 15, par. 10. He was sentenced to banishment from the colonies, and, finally, to avoid arrest, he was forced to flee, amid the cold and storms of winter, into the unbroken forest.

"For fourteen weeks," he says, "I was sorely tossed in a bitter season, not knowing what bread or bed did mean." But "the ravens fed me in the wilderness," and a hollow tree often served him for a shelter.—Martyn, vol. 5, pp. 349, 350. Thus he continued his painful flight through the snow and the trackless forest, until he found refuge with an Indian tribe whose confidence and affection he had won while endeavoring to teach them the truths of the gospel.

Making his way at last, after months of change and wandering, to the shores of Narragansett Bay, he there laid the foundation of the first state of modern times that in the fullest sense recognized the right of religious freedom. The fundamental principle of Roger Williams's colony was "that every man should have liberty to worship God according to the light of his own conscience."—*Ibid.*, vol. 5, p. 354. His little state, Rhode Island, became the asylum of the oppressed, and it increased and prospered until its foundation principles—civil and religious liberty—became the cornerstones of the American Republic.

In that grand old document which our forefathers set forth as their bill of rights—the Declaration of Independence—they declared: "We hold these truths to be self-evident, that all men are created equal; that they are endowed by their Creator with certain unalienable rights; that among these are life, liberty, and the pursuit of happiness." And the Constitution guarantees, in the most explicit terms, the inviolability of conscience: "No religious test shall ever be required as a qualification to any office of public trust under the United States." "Congress shall make no law respecting an establishment of religion, or prohibiting the free exercise thereof."

"The framers of the Constitution recognized the eternal principle that man's relation with his God is above human legislation, and his rights of conscience inalienable. Reasoning was not necessary to establish this truth; we are conscious of it in our own bosoms. It is this consciousness which, in defiance of human laws, has sustained so many martyrs in tortures and flames. They felt that their duty to God was superior to human enactments, and that man could exercise no authority over their consciences. It is an inborn principle which nothing can eradicate."—Congressional documents (U.S.A.), serial No. 200, document No. 271.

As the tidings spread through the countries of Europe, of a land where every man might enjoy the fruit of his own labor and obey the convictions of his own conscience, thousands flocked to the shores of the New World. Colonies rapidly multiplied. "Massachusetts, by special law, offered free welcome and aid, at the public cost, to Christians of any nationality who might fly beyond the Atlantic 'to escape from wars or famine, or the oppression of their persecutors.' Thus the fugitive and the downtrodden were, by statute, made the guests of the commonwealth."—Martyn, vol. 5, p. 417. In twenty years from the first landing at Plymouth, as many thousand Pilgrims were settled in New England.

To secure the object which they sought, "they were content to earn a bare subsistence by a life of frugality and toil. They asked nothing from the soil but the reasonable returns of their own labor. No golden vision threw a deceitful halo around their path. ... They were content with the slow but steady progress of their social polity. They patiently endured the privations of the wilderness, watering the tree of liberty with their tears, and with the sweat of their brow, till it took deep root in the land."

The Bible was held as the foundation of faith, the source of wisdom, and the charter of liberty. Its principles were diligently taught in the home, in the school, and in the church, and its fruits were manifest in thrift, intelligence, purity, and temperance. One might be for years a dweller in the Puritan settlement, "and not see a drunkard, or hear an oath, or meet a beggar."—Bancroft, pt. 1, ch. 19, par. 25. It was demonstrated that the principles of the Bible are the surest safeguards of national greatness. The feeble and isolated colonies grew to a confederation of powerful states, and the world marked with wonder the peace and prosperity of "a church without a pope, and a state without a king."

But continually increasing numbers were attracted to the shores of America, actuated by motives widely different from those of the first Pilgrims. Though the primitive faith and purity exerted a widespread and molding power, yet its influence became less and less as the numbers increased of those who sought only worldly advantage.

The regulation adopted by the early colonists, of permitting only members of the church to vote or to hold office in the civil government, led to most pernicious results. This measure had been accepted as a means of preserving the purity of the state, but it resulted in the corruption of the church. A profession of religion being the condition of suffrage and officeholding, many, actuated solely by motives of worldly policy, united with the church without a change of heart. Thus the churches came to consist, to a considerable extent, of unconverted persons; and even in the ministry were those who not only held errors of doctrine, but who were ignorant of the renewing power of the Holy Spirit. Thus again was demonstrated the evil results, so often witnessed in the history of the church from the days of Constantine to the present, of attempting to build up the church by the aid of the state, of appealing to the secular power in support of the gospel of Him who declared: "My kingdom is not of this world." John 18:36. The union of the church with the state, be the degree ever so slight, while it may appear to bring the world nearer to the church, does in reality but bring the church nearer to the world.

The great principle so nobly advocated by Robinson and Roger Williams, that truth is progressive, that Christians should stand ready to accept all the light which may shine from God's holy word, was lost sight of by their descendants. The Protestant churches of America,—and those of Europe as well,—so highly favored in receiving the blessings of the Reformation, failed to press forward in the path of reform. Though a few faithful men arose, from time to time, to proclaim new truth and expose long-cherished error, the majority, like the Jews in Christ's day or the papists in the time of Luther, were content to believe as their fathers had believed and to live as they had lived. Therefore religion again degenerated into formalism; and errors and superstitions which would have been cast aside had the church continued to walk in the light of God's word, were retained and cherished. Thus the spirit inspired by the Reformation gradually died out, until there was almost as great need of reform in the Protestant churches as in the Roman Church in the time of Luther. There was the same worldliness and spiritual stupor, a similar reverence for the opinions of men, and substitution of human theories for the teachings of God's word.

The wide circulation of the Bible in the early part of the nineteenth century, and the great light thus shed upon the world, was not followed by a corresponding advance in knowledge of revealed truth, or in experimental religion. Satan could not, as in former ages, keep God's word from the people; it had been placed within the reach of all; but in order still to accomplish his object, he led many to value it but lightly. Men neglected to search the Scriptures, and thus they continued to accept false interpretations, and to cherish doctrines which had no foundation in the Bible.

Seeing the failure of his efforts to crush out the truth by persecution, Satan had again resorted to the plan of compromise which led to the great apostasy and the formation of the Church of Rome. He had induced Christians to ally themselves, not now with pagans, but with those who, by their devotion to the things of this world, had proved themselves to be as truly idolaters as were the worshipers of graven images. And the results of this union were no less pernicious now than in former ages; pride and extravagance were fostered under the guise of religion, and the churches became corrupted. Satan continued to pervert the doctrines of the Bible, and traditions that were to ruin millions were taking deep root. The church was upholding and defending these traditions, instead of contending for "the faith which was once delivered unto the saints." Thus were degraded the principles for which the Reformers had done and suffered so much.

Two

—Heralds of the Morning—

One of the most solemn and yet most glorious truths revealed in the Bible is that of Christ's second coming to complete the great work of redemption. To God's pilgrim people, so long left to sojourn in "the region and shadow of death," a precious, joy-inspiring hope is given in the promise of His appearing, who is "the resurrection and the life," to "bring home again His banished." The doctrine of the second advent is the very keynote of the Sacred Scriptures. From the day when the first pair turned their sorrowing steps from Eden, the children of faith have waited the coming of the Promised One to break the destroyer's power and bring them again to the lost Paradise. Holy men of old looked forward to the advent of the Messiah in glory, as the consummation of their hope. Enoch, only the seventh in descent from them that dwelt in Eden, he who for three centuries on earth walked with his God, was permitted to behold from afar the coming of the Deliverer. "Behold," he declared, "the Lord cometh with ten thousands of His saints, to execute judgment upon all." Jude 14, 15. The patriarch Job in the night of his affliction exclaimed with unshaken trust: "I know that my Redeemer liveth, and that He shall stand at the latter day upon the earth: … in my flesh shall I see God: whom I shall see for myself, and mine eyes shall behold, and not another." Job 19:25-27.

The coming of Christ to usher in the reign of righteousness has inspired the most sublime and impassioned utterances of the sacred writers. The poets and prophets of the Bible have dwelt upon it in words glowing with celestial fire. The psalmist sang of the power and majesty of Israel's King: "Out of Zion, the perfection of beauty, God hath shined. Our God shall come, and shall not keep silence. … He shall call to the heavens from above, and to the earth, that He may judge His people." Psalm 50:2-4. "Let the heavens rejoice, and let the earth be glad … before the Lord: for He cometh, for He cometh to judge the earth: He shall judge the world with righteousness, and the people with His truth." Psalm 96:11-13.

Said the prophet Isaiah: "Awake and sing, ye that dwell in dust: for thy dew is as the dew of herbs, and the earth shall cast out the dead." "Thy dead men shall live, together with my dead body shall they arise." "He will swallow up death in victory; and the Lord God will wipe away tears from off all faces; and the rebuke of His people shall He take away from off all the earth: for the Lord hath spoken it. And it shall be said in that day, Lo, this is our God; we have waited for Him, and He will save us: this is the Lord; we have waited for Him, we will be glad and rejoice in His salvation." Isaiah 26:19; 25:8, 9.

And Habakkuk, rapt in holy vision, beheld His appearing. "God came from Teman, and the Holy One from Mount Paran. His glory covered the heavens, and the earth was full of His praise. And His brightness was as the light." "He stood, and measured the earth: He beheld, and drove asunder the nations; and the everlasting mountains were scattered, the perpetual hills did bow: His ways are everlasting." "Thou didst ride upon Thine horses and Thy chariots of salvation." "The mountains saw Thee, and they trembled: … the deep uttered his voice, and lifted up his hands on high. The sun and moon stood still in their habitation: at the light of Thine arrows they went, and at the shining of Thy glittering spear." "Thou wentest forth for the salvation of Thy people, even for salvation with Thine anointed." Habakkuk 3:3, 4, 6, 8, 10, 11, 13.

When the Saviour was about to be separated from His disciples, He comforted them in their sorrow with the assurance that He would come again: "Let not your heart be troubled. … In My Father's house are many mansions. … I go to prepare a place for you. And if I go and prepare a place for you, I will come again, and receive you unto Myself." John 14:1-3. "The Son of man shall come in His glory, and all the holy angels with Him." "Then shall He sit upon the throne of His glory: and before Him shall be gathered all nations." Matthew 25:31, 32.

The angels who lingered upon Olivet after Christ's ascension repeated to the disciples the promise of His return: "This *same* Jesus, which is taken up from you into heaven, shall *so* come in like manner as ye have seen Him go into heaven." Acts 1:11. And the apostle Paul, speaking by the Spirit of Inspiration, testified: "The Lord *Himself* shall descend from heaven with a shout, with the voice of the Archangel, and with the trump of God." 1 Thessalonians 4:16. Says the prophet of Patmos: "Behold, He cometh with clouds; and every eye shall see Him." Revelation 1:7.

About His coming cluster the glories of that "restitution of all things, which God hath spoken by the mouth of all His holy prophets since the world began." Acts 3:21. Then the long-continued rule of evil shall be broken; "the kingdoms of this world" will become "the kingdoms of our Lord, and of His Christ; and He shall reign for ever and ever." Revelation 11:15. "The glory of the Lord shall be revealed, and all flesh shall see it together." "The Lord God will cause righteousness and praise to spring forth before all the nations." He shall be "for a crown of glory, and for a diadem of beauty, unto the residue of His people." Isaiah 40:5; 61:11; 28:5.

It is then that the peaceful and long-desired kingdom of the Messiah shall be established under the whole heaven. "The Lord shall comfort Zion: He will comfort all her waste places; and He will make her wilderness like Eden, and her desert like the garden of the Lord." "The glory of Lebanon shall be given unto it, the excellency of Carmel and Sharon." "Thou shalt no more be termed Forsaken; neither shall thy land any more be termed Desolate: but thou shalt be called My Delight, and thy land Beulah." "As the bridegroom rejoiceth over the bride, so shall thy God rejoice over thee." Isaiah 51:3; 35:2; 62:4, 5, margin.

The coming of the Lord has been in all ages the hope of His true followers. The Saviour's parting promise upon Olivet, that He would come again, lighted up the future for His disciples, filling their hearts with joy and hope that sorrow could not quench nor trials dim. Amid suffering and persecution, the "appearing of the great God and our Saviour Jesus Christ" was the "blessed hope." When the Thessalonian Christians were filled with grief as they buried their loved ones, who had hoped to live to witness the coming of the Lord, Paul, their teacher, pointed them to the resurrection, to take place at the Saviour's advent. Then the dead in Christ should rise, and together with the living be caught up to meet the Lord in the air. "And so," he said, "shall we ever be with the Lord. Wherefore comfort one another with these words." 1 Thessalonians 4:16-18.

On rocky Patmos the beloved disciple hears the promise, "Surely I come quickly," and his longing response voices the prayer of the church in all her pilgrimage, "Even so, come, Lord Jesus." Revelation 22:20.

From the dungeon, the stake, the scaffold, where saints and martyrs witnessed for the truth, comes down the centuries the utterance of their faith and hope. Being "assured of His personal resurrection, and consequently of their own at His coming, for this cause," says one of these Christians, "they despised death, and were found to be above it."—Daniel T. Taylor, *The Reign of Christ on Earth: or, The Voice of the Church in All Ages*, page 33. They were willing to go down to the grave, that they might "rise free."—*Ibid.*, page 54. They looked for the "Lord to come from heaven in the clouds with the glory of His Father," "bringing to the just the times of the kingdom." The Waldenses cherished the same faith.—*Ibid.*, pages 129-132. Wycliffe looked forward to the Redeemer's appearing as the hope of the church.— *Ibid.*, pages 132-134.

Luther declared: "I persuade myself verily, that the day of judgment will not be absent full three hundred years. God will not, cannot, suffer this wicked world much longer." "The great day is drawing near in which the kingdom of abominations shall be overthrown."—*Ibid.*, pages 158, 134.

"This aged world is not far from its end," said Melanchthon. Calvin bids Christians "not to hesitate, ardently desiring the day of Christ's coming as of all events most auspicious;" and declares that "the whole family of the faithful will keep in view that day." "We must hunger after Christ, we must seek, contemplate," he says, "till the dawning of that great day, when our Lord will fully manifest the glory of His kingdom."—*Ibid.*, pages 158, 134.

"Has not the Lord Jesus carried up our flesh into heaven?" said Knox, the Scotch Reformer, "and shall He not return? We know that He shall return, and that with expedition." Ridley and Latimer, who laid down their lives for the truth, looked in faith for the Lord's coming. Ridley wrote: "The world without doubt—this I do believe, and therefore I say it—draws to an end. Let us with John, the servant of God, cry in our hearts unto our Saviour Christ, Come, Lord Jesus, come."—*Ibid.*, pages 151, 145.

"The thoughts of the coming of the Lord," said Baxter, "are most sweet and joyful to me."—Richard Baxter, *Works*, vol. 17, p. 555. "It is the work of faith and the character of His saints to love His appearing and to look for that blessed hope." "If death be the last enemy to be destroyed at the resurrection, we may learn how earnestly believers should long and pray for the second coming of Christ, when this full and final conquest shall be made."—*Ibid.*, vol. 17, p. 500. "This is the day that all believers should long, and hope, and wait for, as being the accomplishment of all the work of their redemption, and all the desires and endeavors of their souls." "Hasten, O Lord, this blessed day!"—*Ibid.*, vol. 17, pp. 182, 183. Such was the hope of the apostolic church, of the "church in the wilderness," and of the Reformers.

Prophecy not only foretells the manner and object of Christ's coming, but presents tokens by which men are to know when it is near. Said Jesus: "There shall be signs in the sun, and in the moon, and in the stars." Luke 21:25. "The sun shall be darkened, and the moon shall not give her light, and the stars of heaven shall fall, and the powers that are in heaven shall be shaken. And then shall they see the Son of man coming in the clouds with great power and glory." Mark 13:24-26. The revelator thus describes the first of the signs to precede the second advent: "There was a great earthquake; and the sun became black as sackcloth of hair, and the moon became as blood." Revelation 6:12.

These signs were witnessed before the opening of the nineteenth century. In fulfillment of this prophecy there occurred, in the year 1755, the most terrible earthquake that has ever been recorded. Though commonly known as the earthquake of Lisbon, it extended to the greater part of Europe, Africa, and America. It was felt in Greenland, in the West Indies, in the island of Madeira, in Norway and Sweden, Great Britain and Ireland. It pervaded an extent of not less than four million square miles. In Africa the shock was almost as severe as in Europe. A great part of Algiers was destroyed; and a short distance from Morocco, a village containing eight or ten thousand inhabitants was swallowed up. A vast wave swept over the coast of Spain and Africa engulfing cities and causing great destruction.

It was in Spain and Portugal that the shock manifested its extreme violence. At Cadiz the inflowing wave was said to be sixty feet high. Mountains, "some of the largest in Portugal, were impetuously shaken, as it were, from their very foundations, and some of them opened at their summits, which were split and rent in a wonderful manner, huge masses of them being thrown down into the adjacent valleys. Flames are related to have issued from these mountains."— Sir Charles Lyell, *Principles of Geology*, page 495.

At Lisbon "a sound of thunder was heard underground, and immediately afterwards a violent shock threw down the greater part of that city. In the course of about six minutes sixty thousand persons perished. The sea first retired, and laid the bar dry; it then rolled in, rising fifty feet or more above its ordinary level." "Among other extraordinary events related to have occurred at Lisbon during the catastrophe, was the subsidence of a new quay, built entirely of marble, at an immense expense. A great concourse of people had collected there for safety, as a spot where they might be beyond the reach of falling ruins; but suddenly the quay sank down with all the people on it, and not one of the dead bodies ever floated to the surface."—*Ibid.,* page 495.

"The shock" of the earthquake "was instantly followed by the fall of every church and convent, almost all the large public buildings, and more than one fourth of the houses. In about two hours after the shock, fires broke out in different quarters, and raged with such violence for the space of nearly three days, that the city was completely desolated. The earthquake happened on a holyday, when the churches and convents were full of people, very few of whom escaped."—*Encyclopedia Americana,* art. "Lisbon," note (ed. 1831). "The terror of the people was beyond description. Nobody wept; it was beyond tears. They ran hither and thither, delirious with horror and astonishment, beating their faces and breasts, crying, '*Misericordia! the world's at an end!*' Mothers forgot their children, and ran about loaded with crucifixed images. Unfortunately, many ran to the churches for protection; but in vain was the sacrament exposed; in vain did the poor creatures embrace the altars; images, priests, and people were buried in one common ruin." It has been estimated that ninety thousand persons lost their lives on that fatal day.

Twenty-five years later appeared the next sign mentioned in the prophecy—the darkening of the sun and moon. What rendered this more striking was the fact that the time of its fulfillment had been definitely pointed out. In the Saviour's conversation with His disciples upon Olivet, after describing the long period of trial for the church,—the 1,260 years of papal persecution, concerning which He had promised that the tribulation should be shortened,—He thus mentioned certain events to precede His coming, and fixed the time when the first of these should be witnessed: "In those days, after that tribulation, the sun shall be darkened, and the moon shall not give her light." Mark 13:24. The 1,260 days, or years, terminated in 1798. A quarter of a century earlier, persecution had almost wholly ceased. Following this persecution, according to the words of Christ, the sun was to be darkened. On the 19th of May, 1780, this prophecy was fulfilled.

"Almost, if not altogether alone, as the most mysterious and as yet unexplained phenomenon of its kind, ... stands the dark day of

May 19, 1780,—a most unaccountable darkening of the whole visible heavens and atmosphere in New England."—R. M. Devens, *Our First Century*, page 89.

An eyewitness living in Massachusetts describes the event as follows: "In the morning the sun rose clear, but was soon overcast. The clouds became lowery, and from them, black and ominous, as they soon appeared, lightning flashed, thunder rolled, and a little rain fell. Toward nine o'clock, the clouds became thinner, and assumed a brassy or coppery appearance, and earth, rocks, trees, buildings, water, and persons were changed by this strange, unearthly light. A few minutes later, a heavy black cloud spread over the entire sky except a narrow rim at the horizon, and it was as dark as it usually is at nine o'clock on a summer evening. ...

"Fear, anxiety, and awe gradually filled the minds of the people. Women stood at the door, looking out upon the dark landscape; men returned from their labor in the fields; the carpenter left his tools, the blacksmith his forge, the tradesman his counter. Schools were dismissed, and tremblingly the children fled homeward. Travelers put up at the nearest farmhouse. 'What is coming?' queried every lip and heart. It seemed as if a hurricane was about to dash across the land, or as if it was the day of the consummation of all things.

"Candles were used; and hearth fires shone as brightly as on a moonless evening in autumn. ... Fowls retired to their roosts and went to sleep, cattle gathered at the pasture bars and lowed, frogs peeped, birds sang their evening songs, and bats flew about. But the human knew that night had not come. ...

"Dr. Nathanael Whittaker, pastor of the Tabernacle church in Salem, held religious services in the meeting-house, and preached a sermon in which he maintained that the darkness was supernatural. Congregations came together in many other places. The texts for the extemporaneous sermons were invariably those that seemed to indicate that the darkness was consonant with Scriptural prophecy. ... The darkness was most dense shortly after eleven o'clock."—*The Essex Antiquarian*, April, 1899, vol. 3, No. 4, pp. 53, 54. "In most parts of the country it was so great in the daytime, that the people could not tell the hour by either watch or clock, nor dine, nor manage their domestic business, without the light of candles. ...

"The extent of this darkness was extraordinary. It was observed as far east as Falmouth. To the westward it reached to the farthest part of

Connecticut, and to Albany. To the southward, it was observed along the seacoasts; and to the north as far as the American settlements extend."—William Gordon, *History of the Rise, Progress, and Establishment of the Independence of the U.S.A.*, vol. 3, p. 57.

The intense darkness of the day was succeeded, an hour or two before evening, by a partially clear sky, and the sun appeared, though it was still obscured by the black, heavy mist. "After sundown, the clouds came again overhead, and it grew dark very fast." "Nor was the darkness of the night less uncommon and terrifying than that of the day; notwithstanding there was almost a full moon, no object was discernible but by the help of some artificial light, which, when seen from the neighboring houses and other places at a distance, appeared through a kind of Egyptian darkness which seemed almost impervious to the rays."—Isaiah Thomas, *Massachusetts Spy; or, American Oracle of Liberty*, vol. 10, No. 472 (May 25, 1780). Said an eyewitness of the scene: "I could not help conceiving at the time, that if every luminous body in the universe had been shrouded in impenetrable shades, or struck out of existence, the darkness could not have been more complete."—Letter by Dr. Samuel Tenney, of Exeter, New Hampshire, December, 1785 (in *Massachusetts Historical Society Collections*, 1792, 1st series, vol. 1, p. 97). Though at nine o'clock that night the moon rose to the full, "it had not the least effect to dispel the deathlike shadows." After midnight the darkness disappeared, and the moon, when first visible, had the appearance of blood.

May 19, 1780, stands in history as "The Dark Day." Since the time of Moses no period of darkness of equal density, extent, and duration, has ever been recorded. The description of this event, as given by eyewitnesses, is but an echo of the words of the Lord, recorded by the prophet Joel, twenty-five hundred years previous to their fulfillment: "The sun shall be turned into darkness, and the moon into blood, before the great and terrible day of the Lord come." Joel 2:31.

Christ had bidden His people watch for the signs of His advent and rejoice as they should behold the tokens of their coming King. "When these things begin to come to pass," He said, "then look up, and lift up your heads; for your redemption draweth nigh." He pointed His followers to the budding trees of spring, and said: "When they now shoot forth, ye see and know of your own selves that summer is now nigh at hand. So likewise ye, when ye see these things come to pass, know ye that the kingdom of God is nigh at hand." Luke 21:28, 30, 31.

But as the spirit of humility and devotion in the church had given place to pride and formalism, love for Christ and faith in His coming had grown cold. Absorbed in worldliness and pleasure seeking, the professed people of God were blinded to the Saviour's instructions concerning the signs of His appearing. The doctrine of the second advent had been neglected; the scriptures relating to it were obscured by misinterpretation, until it was, to a great extent, ignored and forgotten. Especially was this the case in the churches of America. The freedom and comfort enjoyed by all classes of society, the ambitious desire for wealth and luxury, begetting an absorbing devotion to money-making, the eager rush for popularity and power, which seemed to be within the reach of all, led men to center their interests and hopes on the things of this life, and to put far in the future that solemn day when the present order of things should pass away.

When the Saviour pointed out to His followers the signs of His return, He foretold the state of backsliding that would exist just prior to His second advent. There would be, as in the days of Noah, the activity and stir of worldly business and pleasure seeking—buying, selling, planting, building, marrying, and giving in marriage—with forgetfulness of God and the future life. For those living at this time, Christ's admonition is: "Take heed to yourselves, lest at any time your hearts be overcharged with surfeiting, and drunkenness, and cares of this life, and so that day come upon you unawares." "Watch ye therefore, and pray always, that ye may be accounted worthy to escape all these things that shall come to pass, and to stand before the Son of man." Luke 21:34, 36.

The condition of the church at this time is pointed out in the Saviour's words in the Revelation: "Thou hast a name that thou livest, and art dead." And to those who refuse to arouse from their careless security, the solemn warning is addressed: "If therefore thou shalt not watch, I will come on thee as a thief, and thou shalt not know what hour I will come upon thee." Revelation 3:1, 3.

It was needful that men should be awakened to their danger; that they should be roused to prepare for the solemn events connected with the close of probation. The prophet of God declares: "The day of the Lord is great and very terrible; and who can abide it?" Who shall stand when He appeareth who is "of purer eyes than to behold evil," and cannot "look on iniquity"? Joel 2:11; Habakkuk 1:13. To them that cry, "My God, we know Thee," yet have transgressed His covenant, and hastened after another god, hiding iniquity in their hearts, and loving the paths of unrighteousness—to these the day of the Lord is "darkness, and not light, even very dark, and no brightness in it." Hosea 8:2, 1; Psalm 16;4; Amos 5:20. "It shall come to pass at that time," saith the Lord, "that I will search Jerusalem with candles, and punish the men that are settled on their lees: that say in their heart, The Lord will not do good, neither will He do evil." Zephaniah 1:12. "I will punish the world for their evil, and the wicked for their iniquity; and I will cause the arrogancy of the proud to cease, and will lay low the haughtiness of the terrible." Isaiah 13:11. "Neither their silver nor their gold shall be able to deliver them;" "their goods shall become a booty, and their houses a desolation." Zephaniah 1:18, 13.

The prophet Jeremiah, looking forward to this fearful time, exclaimed: "I am pained at my very heart. ... I cannot hold my peace, because thou hast heard, O my soul, the sound of the trumpet, the alarm of war. Destruction upon destruction is cried." Jeremiah 4:19, 20.

"That day is a day of wrath, a day of trouble and distress, a day of wasteness and desolation, a day of darkness and gloominess, a day of clouds and thick darkness, a day of the trumpet and alarm." Zephaniah 1:15, 16. "Behold, the day of the Lord cometh, ... to lay the land desolate: and He shall destroy the sinners thereof out of it." Isaiah 13:9.

In view of that great day the word of God, in the most solemn and impressive language, calls upon His people to arouse from their spiritual lethargy and to seek His face with repentance and humiliation: "Blow ye the trumpet in Zion, and sound an alarm in My holy mountain: let all the inhabitants of the land tremble: for the day of the Lord cometh, for it is nigh at hand." "Sanctify a fast, call a solemn assembly: gather the people, sanctify the congregation, assemble the elders, gather the children: ... let the bridegroom go forth of his chamber, and the bride out of her closet. Let the priests, the ministers of the Lord, weep between the porch and the altar." "Turn ye even to Me with all your heart, and with fasting, and with weeping, and with mourning: and rend your heart, and not your garments, and turn unto the Lord your God: for He is gracious and merciful, slow to anger, and of great kindness." Joel 2:1, 15-17, 12, 13.

To prepare a people to stand in the day of God, a great work of reform was to be accomplished. God saw that many of His professed people were not building for eternity, and in His mercy He was about to send a message of warning to arouse them from their stupor and lead them to make ready for the coming of the Lord.

This warning is brought to view in Revelation 14. Here is a threefold message represented as proclaimed by heavenly beings and immediately followed by the coming of the Son of man to reap "the harvest of the earth." The first of these warnings announces the approaching judgment. The prophet beheld an angel flying "in the midst of heaven, having the everlasting gospel to preach unto them that dwell on the earth, and to every nation, and kindred, and tongue, and people, saying with a loud voice, Fear God, and give glory to Him; for the hour of His judgment is come: and worship Him that made heaven, and earth, and the sea, and the fountains of waters." Revelation 14:6, 7.

This message is declared to be a part of "the everlasting gospel." The work of preaching the gospel has not been committed to angels, but has been entrusted to men. Holy angels have been employed in directing this work, they have in charge the great movements for the salvation of men; but the actual proclamation of the gospel is performed by the servants of Christ upon the earth.

Faithful men, who were obedient to the promptings of God's Spirit and the teachings of His word, were to proclaim this warning to the world. They were those who had taken heed to the "sure word of prophecy," the "light that shineth in a dark place, until the day dawn, and the daystar arise." 2 Peter 1:19. They had been seeking the knowledge of God more than all hid treasures, counting it "better than the merchandise of silver, and the gain thereof than fine gold." Proverbs 3:14. And the Lord revealed to them the great things of the kingdom. "The secret of the Lord is with them that fear Him; and He will show them His covenant." Psalm 25:14.

It was not the scholarly theologians who had an understanding of this truth, and engaged in its proclamation. Had these been faithful watchmen, diligently and prayerfully searching the Scriptures, they would have known the time of night; the prophecies would have opened to them the events about to take place. But they did not occupy this position, and the message was given by humbler men. Said Jesus: "Walk while ye have the light, lest darkness come upon you." John 12:35. Those who turn away from the light which God has given, or who neglect to seek it when it is within their reach, are left in darkness. But the Saviour declares: "He that followeth Me shall not walk in darkness, but shall have the light of life." John 8:12. Whoever is with singleness of purpose seeking to do God's will, earnestly heeding the light already given, will receive greater light; to that soul some star of heavenly radiance will be sent to guide him into all truth.

At the time of Christ's first advent the priests and scribes of the Holy City, to whom were entrusted the oracles of God, might have discerned the signs of the times and proclaimed the coming of the Promised One. The prophecy of Micah designated His birthplace; Daniel specified the time of His advent. Micah 5:2; Daniel 9:25. God committed these prophecies to the Jewish leaders; they were without excuse if they did not know and declare to the people that the Messiah's coming was at hand. Their ignorance was the result of sinful neglect. The Jews were building monuments for the slain prophets of God, while by their deference to the great men of earth they were paying homage to the servants of Satan. Absorbed in their ambitious strife for place and power among men, they lost sight of the divine honors proffered them by the King of heaven.

With profound and reverent interest the elders of Israel should have been studying the place, the time, the circumstances, of the greatest event in the world's history—the coming of the Son of God to accomplish the redemption of man. All the people should have been watching and waiting that they might be among the first to welcome the world's Redeemer. But, lo, at Bethlehem two weary travelers from the hills of Nazareth traverse the whole length of the narrow street to the eastern extremity of the town, vainly seeking a place of rest and shelter for the night. No doors are open to receive them. In a wretched hovel prepared for cattle, they at last find refuge, and there the Saviour of the world is born.

Heavenly angels had seen the glory which the Son of God shared with the Father before the world was, and they had looked forward with intense interest to His appearing on earth as an event fraught with the greatest joy to all people. Angels were appointed to carry the glad tidings to those who were prepared to receive it and who would joyfully make it known to the inhabitants of the earth. Christ had stooped to take upon Himself man's nature; He was to bear an infinite weight of woe as He should make His soul an offering for sin; yet angels desired that even in His humiliation the Son of the Highest might appear before men with a dignity and glory befitting His character. Would the great men of earth assemble at Israel's capital to greet His coming? Would legions of angels present Him to the expectant company?

An angel visits the earth to see who are prepared to welcome Jesus. But he can discern no tokens of expectancy. He hears no voice of praise and triumph that the period of Messiah's coming is at hand. The angel hovers for a time over the chosen city and the temple where the divine presence has been manifested for ages; but even here is the same indifference. The priests, in their pomp and pride, are offering polluted sacrifices in the temple. The Pharisees are with loud voices addressing the people or making boastful prayers at the corners of the streets. In the palaces of kings, in the assemblies of philosophers, in the schools of the rabbis, all are alike unmindful of the wondrous fact which has filled all heaven with joy and praise—that the Redeemer of men is about to appear upon the earth.

There is no evidence that Christ is expected, and no preparation for the Prince of life. In amazement the celestial messenger is about to return to heaven with the shameful tidings, when he discovers a group of shepherds who are watching their flocks by night, and, as they gaze into the starry heavens, are contemplating the prophecy of a Messiah to come to earth, and longing for the advent of the world's Redeemer. Here is a company that is prepared to receive the heavenly message. And suddenly the angel of the Lord appears, declaring the good tidings of great joy. Celestial glory floods all the plain, an innumerable company of angels is revealed, and as if the joy were too great for one messenger to bring from heaven, a multitude of voices break forth in the anthem which all the nations of the saved shall one day sing: "Glory to God in the highest, and on earth peace, good will toward men." Luke 2:14.

Oh, what a lesson is this wonderful story of Bethlehem! How it rebukes our unbelief, our pride and self-sufficiency. How it warns us to beware, lest by our criminal indifference we also fail to discern the signs of the times, and therefore know not the day of our visitation.

It was not alone upon the hills of Judea, not among the lowly shepherds only, that angels found the watchers for Messiah's coming. In the land of the heathen also were those that looked for Him; they were wise men, rich and noble, the philosophers of the East. Students of nature, the Magi had seen God in His handiwork. From the Hebrew Scriptures they had learned of the Star to arise out of Jacob, and with eager desire they awaited His coming, who should be not only the "Consolation of Israel," but a "Light to lighten the Gentiles," and "for salvation unto the ends of the earth." Luke 2:25, 32; Acts 13:47. They were seekers for light, and light from the throne of God illumined the path for their feet. While the priests and rabbis of Jerusalem, the appointed guardians and expounders of the truth, were shrouded in darkness, the Heaven-sent star guided these Gentile strangers to the birthplace of the newborn King.

It is "unto them that look for Him" that Christ is to "appear the second time without sin unto salvation." Hebrews 9:28. Like the tidings of the Saviour's birth, the message of the second advent was not committed to the religious leaders of the people. They had failed to preserve their connection with God, and had refused light from heaven; therefore they were not of the number described by the apostle Paul: "But ye, brethren, are not in darkness, that that day should overtake you as a thief. Ye are all the children of light, and the children of the day: we are not of the night, nor of darkness." 1 Thessalonians 5:4, 5.

The watchmen upon the walls of Zion should have been the first to catch the tidings of the Saviour's advent, the first to lift their voices to proclaim Him near, the first to warn the people to prepare for His coming. But they were at ease, dreaming of peace and safety, while the people were asleep in their sins. Jesus saw His church, like the barren fig tree, covered with pretentious leaves, yet destitute of precious fruit. There was a boastful observance of the forms of religion, while the spirit of true humility, penitence, and faith—which alone could render the service acceptable to God—was lacking. Instead of the graces of the Spirit there were manifested pride, formalism, vainglory, selfishness, and oppression. A backsliding church closed their eyes to the signs of the times. God did not forsake them, or suffer His faithfulness to fail; but they departed from Him, and separated themselves from His love. As they refused to comply with the conditions, His promises were not fulfilled to them.

Such is the sure result of neglect to appreciate and improve the light and privileges which God bestows. Unless the church will follow on in His opening providence, accepting every ray of light, performing every duty which may be revealed, religion will inevitably degenerate into the observance of forms, and the spirit of vital godliness will disappear. This truth has been repeatedly illustrated in the history of the church. God requires of His people works of faith and obedience corresponding to the blessings and privileges bestowed. Obedience requires a sacrifice and involves a cross; and this is why so many of the professed followers of Christ refused to receive the light from heaven, and, like the Jews of old, knew not the time of their visitation. Luke 19:44. Because of their pride and unbelief the Lord passed them by and revealed His truth to those who, like the shepherds of Bethlehem and the Eastern Magi, had given heed to all the light they had received.

Three

—An American Reformer—

A n upright, honest-hearted farmer, who had been led to doubt the divine authority of the Scriptures, yet who sincerely desired to know the truth, was the man specially chosen of God to lead out in the proclamation of Christ's second coming. Like many other reformers, William Miller had in early life battled with poverty and had thus learned the great lessons of energy and self-denial. The members of the family from which he sprang were characterized by an independent, liberty-loving spirit, by capability of endurance, and ardent patriotism—traits which were also prominent in his character. His father was a captain in the army of the Revolution, and to the sacrifices which he made in the struggles and sufferings of that stormy period may be traced the straitened circumstances of Miller's early life.

He had a sound physical constitution, and even in childhood gave evidence of more than ordinary intellectual strength. As he grew older, this became more marked. His mind was active and well developed, and he had a keen thirst for knowledge. Though he did not enjoy the advantages of a collegiate education, his love of study and a habit of careful thought and close criticism rendered him a man of sound judgment and comprehensive views. He possessed an irreproachable moral character and an enviable reputation, being generally esteemed for integrity, thrift, and benevolence. By dint of energy and application he early acquired a competence, though his habits of study were still maintained. He filled various civil and military offices with credit, and the avenues to wealth and honor seemed wide open to him.

His mother was a woman of sterling piety, and in childhood, he had been subject to religious impressions. In early childhood, however, he was thrown into the society of deists, whose influence was the stronger from the fact that they were mostly good citizens and men of humane and benevolent disposition. Living, as they did, in the midst of Christian institutions, their characters had been to some extent molded by their surroundings. For the excellencies which won them respect and confidence they were indebted to the Bible; and yet these good gifts were so perverted as to exert an influence against the word of God. By association with these men, Miller was led to adopt their sentiments. The current interpretations of Scripture presented difficulties which seemed to him insurmountable; yet his new belief, while setting aside the Bible, offered nothing better to take its place, and he remained far from satisfied. He continued to hold these views, however, for about twelve years. But at the age of thirty-four the Holy Spirit impressed his heart with a sense of his condition as a sinner. He found in his former belief no assurance of happiness beyond the grave. The future was dark and gloomy. Referring afterward to his feelings at this time, he said:

"Annihilation was a cold and chilling thought, and accountability was sure destruction to all. The heavens were as brass over my head, and the earth as iron under my feet. Eternity—what was it? And death—why was it? The more I reasoned, the further I was from demonstration. The more I thought, the more scattered were my conclusions. I tried to stop thinking, but my thoughts would not be controlled. I was truly wretched, but did not understand the cause. I murmured and complained, but knew not of whom. I knew that there was a wrong, but knew not how or where to find the right. I mourned, but without hope."

In this state he continued for some months. "Suddenly," he says, "the character of a Saviour was vividly impressed upon my mind. It seemed that there might be a being so good and compassionate as to himself atone for our transgressions, and thereby save us from suffering the penalty of sin. I immediately felt how lovely such a being must be, and imagined that I could cast myself into the arms of, and trust in the mercy of, such a one. But the question arose, How can it be proved that such a being does exist? Aside from the Bible, I found that I could get no evidence of the existence of such a Saviour, or even of a future state. ...

"I saw that the Bible did bring to view just such a Saviour as I needed; and I was perplexed to find how an uninspired book should develop principles so perfectly adapted to the wants of a fallen world. I was constrained to admit that the Scriptures must be a revelation from God. They became my delight; and in Jesus I found a friend. The Saviour

became to me the chiefest among ten thousand; and the Scriptures, which before were dark and contradictory, now became the lamp to my feet and light to my path. My mind became settled and satisfied. I found the Lord God to be a Rock in the midst of the ocean of life. The Bible now became my chief study, and I can truly say, I searched it with great delight. I found the half was never told me. I wondered why I had not seen its beauty and glory before, and marveled that I could have ever rejected it. I found everything revealed that my heart could desire, and a remedy for every disease of the soul. I lost all taste for other reading, and applied my heart to get wisdom from God."
—S. Bliss, *Memoirs of Wm. Miller*, pages 65-67.

Miller publicly professed his faith in the religion which he had despised. But his infidel associates were not slow to bring forward all those arguments which he himself had often urged against the divine authority of the Scriptures. He was not then prepared to answer them; but he reasoned that if the Bible is a revelation from God, it must be consistent with itself; and that as it was given for man's instruction, it must be adapted to his understanding. He determined to study the Scriptures for himself, and ascertain if every apparent contradiction could not be harmonized.

Endeavoring to lay aside all preconceived opinions, and dispensing with commentaries, he compared scripture with scripture by the aid of the marginal references and the concordance. He pursued his study in a regular and methodical manner; beginning with Genesis, and reading verse by verse, he proceeded no faster than the meaning of the several passages so unfolded as to leave him free from all embarrassment. When he found anything obscure, it was his custom to compare it with every other text which seemed to have any reference to the matter under consideration. Every word was permitted to have its proper bearing upon the subject of the text, and if his view of it harmonized with every collateral passage, it ceased to be a difficulty. Thus whenever he met with a passage hard to be understood he found an explanation in some other portion of the Scriptures. As he studied with earnest prayer for divine enlightenment, that which had before appeared dark to his understanding was made clear. He experienced the truth of the psalmist's words: "The entrance of Thy words giveth light; it giveth understanding unto the simple." Psalm 119:130.

With intense interest he studied the books of Daniel and the Revelation, employing the same principles of interpretation as in the other scriptures, and found, to his great joy, that the prophetic symbols could be understood. He saw that the prophecies, so far as they had been fulfilled, had been fulfilled literally; that all the various figures, metaphors, parables, similitudes, etc., were either explained in their immediate connection, or the terms in which they were expressed were defined in other scriptures, and when thus explained, were to be literally understood. "I was thus satisfied," he says, "that the Bible is a system of revealed truths, so clearly and simply given that the wayfaring man, though a fool, need not err therein."—Bliss, page 70. Link after link of the chain of truth rewarded his efforts, as step by step he traced down the great lines of prophecy. Angels of heaven were guiding his mind and opening the Scriptures to his understanding.

Taking the manner in which the prophecies had been fulfilled in the past as a criterion by which to judge of the fulfillment of those which were still future, he became satisfied that the popular view of the spiritual reign of Christ—a temporal millennium before the end of the world—was not sustained by the word of God. This doctrine, pointing to a thousand years of righteousness and peace before the personal coming of the Lord, put far off the terrors of the day of God. But, pleasing though it may be, it is contrary to the teachings of Christ and His apostles, who declared that the wheat and the tares are to grow together until the harvest, the end of the world; that "evil men and seducers shall wax worse and worse;" that "in the last days perilous times shall come;" and that the kingdom of darkness shall continue until the advent of the Lord and shall be consumed with the spirit of His mouth and be destroyed with the brightness of His coming. Matthew 13:30, 38-41; 2 Timothy 3:13, 1; 2 Thessalonians 2:8.

The doctrine of the world's conversion and the spiritual reign of Christ was not held by the apostolic church. It was not generally accepted by Christians until about the beginning of the eighteenth century. Like every other error, its results were evil. It taught men to look far in the future for the coming of the Lord and prevented them from giving heed to the signs heralding His approach. It induced a feeling of confidence and security that was not well founded and led many to neglect the preparation necessary in order to meet their Lord.

Miller found the literal, personal coming of Christ to be plainly taught in the Scriptures. Says Paul: "The Lord Himself shall descend from heaven with a shout, with the voice of the Archangel, and with the trump of God." 1 Thessalonians 4:16. And the Saviour declares: "They shall *see* the Son of man coming in the clouds of heaven with power and great glory." "For as the lightning cometh out of the east, and shineth even unto the west; so shall also the coming of the Son of man be." Matthew 24:30, 27. He is to be accompanied by all the hosts of heaven. "The Son of man shall come in His glory, and all the holy angels with Him." Matthew 25:31. "And He shall send His angels with a great sound of a trumpet, and they shall gather together His elect." Matthew 24:31.

At His coming the righteous dead will be raised, and the righteous living will be changed. "We shall not all sleep," says Paul, "but we shall all be changed, in a moment, in the twinkling of an eye, at the last trump: for the trumpet shall sound, and the dead shall be raised incorruptible, and we shall be changed. For this corruptible must put on incorruption, and this mortal must put on immortality." 1 Corinthians 15:51-53. And in his letter to the Thessalonians, after describing the coming of the Lord, he says: "The dead in Christ shall rise first: then we which are alive and remain shall be caught up together with them in the clouds, to meet the Lord in the air: and so shall we ever be with the Lord." 1 Thessalonians 4:16, 17.

Not until the personal advent of Christ can His people receive the kingdom. The Saviour said: "When the Son of man shall come in His glory, and all the holy angels with Him, then shall He sit upon the throne of His glory: and before Him shall be gathered all nations: and He shall separate them one from another, as a shepherd divideth his sheep from the goats: and He shall set the sheep on His right hand, but the goats on the left. Then shall the King say unto them on His right hand, Come, ye blessed of My Father, inherit the kingdom prepared for you from the foundation of the world." Matthew 25:31-34. We have seen by the scriptures just given that when the Son of man comes, the dead are raised incorruptible and the living are changed. By this great change they are prepared to receive the kingdom; for Paul says: "Flesh and blood cannot inherit the kingdom of God; neither doth corruption inherit incorruption." 1 Corinthians 15:50. Man in his present state is mortal, corruptible; but the kingdom of God will be incorruptible, enduring forever. Therefore man in his present state cannot enter into the kingdom of God. But when Jesus comes, He confers immortality upon His people; and then He calls them to inherit the kingdom of which they have hitherto been only heirs.

These and other scriptures clearly proved to Miller's mind that the events which were generally expected to take place before the coming of Christ, such as the universal reign of peace and the setting up of the kingdom of God upon the earth, were to be subsequent to the second advent. Furthermore, all the signs of the times and the condition of the world corresponded to the prophetic description of the last days. He was forced to the conclusion, from the study of Scripture alone, that the period allotted for the continuance of the earth in its present state was about to close.

"Another kind of evidence that vitally affected my mind," he says, "was the chronology of the Scriptures. ... I found that predicted events, which had been fulfilled in the past, often occurred within a given time. The one hundred and twenty years to the flood (Genesis 6:3); the seven days that were to precede it, with forty days of predicted rain (Genesis 7:4); the four hundred years of the sojourn of Abraham's seed (Genesis 15:13); the three days of the butler's and baker's dreams (Genesis 40:12-20); the seven years of Pharaoh's (Genesis 41:28-54); the forty years in the wilderness (Numbers 14:34); the three and a half years of famine (1 Kings 17:1) [see Luke 4:25;] ... the seventy years' captivity (Jeremiah 25:11); Nebuchadnezzar's seven times (Daniel 4:13-16); and the seven weeks, threescore and two weeks, and the one week, making seventy weeks, determined upon the Jews (Daniel 9:24-27),—the events limited by these times were all once only a matter of prophecy, and were fulfilled in accordance with the predictions."—Bliss, pages 74, 75.

When, therefore, he found, in his study of the Bible, various chronological periods that, according to his understanding of them, extended to the second coming of Christ, he could not but regard them as the "times before appointed," which God had revealed unto His servants. "The secret things," says Moses, "belong unto the Lord our God: but those things which are revealed belong unto us and to our children forever;" and the Lord declares by the prophet Amos, that He "will do nothing, but He revealeth His secret unto His servants the prophets." Deuteronomy 29:29; Amos 3:7. The students of God's word may, then, confidently expect to find the most stupendous event to take place in human history clearly pointed out in the Scriptures of truth.

"As I was fully convinced," says Miller, "that all Scripture given by inspiration of God is profitable (2 Timothy 3:16); that it came not at any time by the will of man, but was written as holy men were moved by the Holy Ghost (2 Peter 1:21), and was written 'for our learning, that we through patience and comfort of the Scriptures might have hope' (Romans 15:4), I could but regard the chronological portions of the Bible as being as much a portion of the word of God, and as much entitled to our serious consideration, as any other portion of the Scriptures. I therefore felt that in endeavoring to comprehend what God had in His mercy seen fit to reveal to us, I had no right to pass over the prophetic periods."—Bliss, page 75.

The prophecy which seemed most clearly to reveal the *time* of the second advent was that of Daniel 8:14: "Unto two thousand and three hundred days; then shall the sanctuary be cleansed." Following his rule of making Scripture its own interpreter, Miller learned that a day in symbolic prophecy represents a year (Numbers 14:34; Ezekiel 4:6); he saw that the period of 2,300 prophetic days, or literal years, would extend far beyond the close of the Jewish dispensation, hence it could not refer to the sanctuary of that dispensation. Miller accepted the generally received view that in the Christian age the earth is the sanctuary, and he therefore understood that the cleansing of the sanctuary foretold in Daniel 8:14 represented the purification of the earth by fire at the second coming of Christ. If, then, the correct starting point could be found for the 2,300 days, he concluded that the time of the second advent could be readily ascertained. Thus would be revealed the time of that great consummation, the time when the present state, with "all its pride and power, pomp and vanity, wickedness and oppression, would come to an end;" when the curse would be "removed from off the earth, death be destroyed, reward be given to the servants of God, the prophets and saints, and them who fear His name, and those be destroyed that destroy the earth."—Bliss, page 76.

With a new and deeper earnestness, Miller continued the examination of the prophecies, whole nights as well as days being devoted to the study of what now appeared of such stupendous importance and all-absorbing interest. In the eighth chapter of Daniel he could find no clue to the starting point of the 2,300 days; the angel Gabriel, though commanded to make Daniel understand the vision, gave him only a partial explanation. As the terrible persecution to befall the church was unfolded to the prophet's vision, physical strength gave way. He could endure no more, and the angel left him for a time. Daniel "fainted, and was sick certain days." "And I was astonished at the vision," he says, "but none understood it."

Yet God had bidden His messenger: "Make this man to understand the vision." That commission must be fulfilled. In obedience to it, the angel, some time afterward, returned to Daniel, saying: "I am now come forth to give thee skill and understanding;" "therefore understand the matter, and consider the vision." Daniel 8:27, 16; 9:22, 23, 25-27. There was one important point in the vision of chapter 8 which had been left unexplained, namely, that relating to time—the period of the 2,300 days; therefore the angel, in resuming his explanation, dwells chiefly upon the subject of time:

"Seventy weeks are determined upon thy people and upon thy Holy City. ... Know therefore and understand, that from the going forth of the commandment to restore and to build Jerusalem unto the Messiah the Prince shall be seven weeks, and threescore and two weeks: the street shall be built again, and the wall, even in troublous times. And after threescore and two weeks shall Messiah be cut off, but not for Himself. ... And He shall confirm the covenant with many for one week: and in the midst of the week He shall cause the sacrifice and the oblation to cease."

The angel had been sent to Daniel for the express purpose of explaining to him the point which he had failed to understand in the vision of the eighth chapter, the statement relative to time—"unto two thousand and three hundred days; then shall the sanctuary be cleansed." After bidding Daniel "understand the matter, and consider the vision," the very first words of the angel are: "Seventy weeks are determined upon thy people and upon thy Holy City." The word here translated "determined" literally signifies "cut off." Seventy weeks, representing 490 years, are declared by the angel to be cut off, as specially pertaining to the Jews. But from what were they cut off? As the 2,300 days was the only period of time mentioned in chapter 8, it must be the period from which the seventy weeks were cut off; the seventy weeks must therefore be a part of the 2,300 days, and the two periods must begin together. The seventy weeks were declared by the angel to date from the going forth of the commandment to restore and build Jerusalem. If the date of this commandment could be found, then the starting point for the great period of the 2,300 days would be ascertained.

In the seventh chapter of Ezra the decree is found. Verses 12-26. In its completest form it was issued by Artaxerxes, king of Persia, 457 B.C. But in Ezra 6:14 the house of the Lord at Jerusalem is said to have been built "according to the commandment ["decree," margin] of

Cyrus, and Darius, and Artaxerxes king of Persia." These three kings, in originating, reaffirming, and completing the decree, brought it to the perfection required by the prophecy to mark the beginning of the 2,300 years. Taking 457 B.C., the time when the decree was completed, as the date of the commandment, every specification of the prophecy concerning the seventy weeks was seen to have been fulfilled.

"From the going forth of the commandment to restore and to build Jerusalem unto the Messiah the Prince shall be seven weeks, and threescore and two weeks"—namely, sixty-nine weeks, or 483 years. The decree of Artaxerxes went into effect in the autumn of 457 B.C. From this date, 483 years extend to the autumn of A.D. 27. At that time this prophecy was fulfilled. The word "Messiah" signifies "the Anointed One." In the autumn of A.D. 27 Christ was baptized by John and received the anointing of the Spirit. The apostle Peter testifies that "God anointed Jesus of Nazareth with the Holy Ghost and with power." Acts 10:38. And the Saviour Himself declared: "The Spirit of the Lord is upon Me, because He hath anointed Me to preach the gospel to the poor." Luke 4:18. After His baptism He went into Galilee, "preaching the gospel of the kingdom of God, and saying, *The time* is fulfilled." Mark 1:14, 15.

"And He shall confirm the covenant with many for one week." The "week" here brought to view is the last one of the seventy; it is the last seven years of the period allotted especially to the Jews. During this time, extending from A.D. 27 to A.D. 34, Christ, at first in person and afterward by His disciples, extended the gospel invitation especially to the Jews. As the apostles went forth with the good tidings of the kingdom, the Saviour's direction was: "Go not into the way of the Gentiles, and into any city of the Samaritans enter ye not: but go rather to the lost sheep of the house of Israel." Matthew 10:5, 6.

"In the midst of the week He shall cause the sacrifice and the oblation to cease." In A.D. 31, three and a half years after His baptism, our Lord was crucified. With the great sacrifice offered upon Calvary, ended that system of offerings which for four thousand years had pointed forward to the Lamb of God. Type had met antitype, and all the sacrifices and oblations of the ceremonial system were there to cease.

The seventy weeks, or 490 years, especially allotted to the Jews, ended, as we have seen, in A.D. 34. At that time, through the action of the Jewish Sanhedrin, the nation sealed its rejection of the gospel by the martyrdom of Stephen and the persecution of the followers of Christ. Then the message of salvation, no longer restricted to the chosen people, was given to the world. The disciples, forced by persecution to flee from Jerusalem, "went everywhere preaching the word." "Philip went down to the city of Samaria, and preached Christ unto them." Peter, divinely guided, opened the gospel to the centurion of Caesarea, the God-fearing Cornelius; and the ardent Paul, won to the faith of Christ, was commissioned to carry the glad tidings "far hence unto the Gentiles." Acts 8:4, 5; 22:21.

Thus far every specification of the prophecies is strikingly fulfilled, and the beginning of the seventy weeks is fixed beyond question at 457 B.C., and their expiration in A.D. 34. From this data there is no difficulty in finding the termination of the 2,300 days. The seventy weeks—490 days—having been cut off from the 2,300, there were 1810 days remaining. After the end of 490 days, the 1810 days were still to be fulfilled. From A.D. 34, 1810 years extend to 1844. Consequently the 2,300 days of Daniel 8:14 terminate in 1844. At the expiration of this great prophetic period, upon the testimony of the angel of God, "the sanctuary shall be cleansed." Thus the time of the cleansing of the sanctuary—which was almost universally believed to take place at the second advent—was definitely pointed out.

Miller and his associates at first believed that the 2,300 days would terminate in the *spring* of 1844, whereas the prophecy points to the *autumn* of that year. The misapprehension of this point brought disappointment and perplexity to those who had fixed upon the earlier date as the time of the Lord's coming. But this did not in the least affect the strength of the argument showing that the 2,300 days terminated in the year 1844, and that the great event represented by the cleansing of the sanctuary must then take place.

Entering upon the study of the Scriptures as he had done, in order to prove that they were a revelation from God, Miller had not, at the outset, the slightest expectation of reaching the conclusion at which he had now arrived. He himself could hardly credit the results of his investigation. But the Scripture evidence was too clear and forcible to be set aside.

He had devoted two years to the study of the Bible, when, in 1818, he reached the solemn conviction that in about twenty-five years Christ would appear for the redemption of His people. "I need not speak," says Miller, "of the joy that filled my heart in view of the delightful prospect, nor of the ardent longings of my soul for a participation in the joys of the redeemed. The Bible was now to me a new book. It was indeed a feast of reason; all that was dark, mystical, or obscure to me in its teachings, had been dissipated from my mind before the clear light that now dawned from its sacred pages; and, oh, how bright and glorious the truth appeared! All the contradictions and inconsistencies I had before found in the word were gone; and although there were many portions of which I was not satisfied I had a full understanding, yet so much light had emanated from it to the illumination of my before darkened mind, that I felt a delight in studying the Scripture which I had not before supposed could be derived from its teachings."—Bliss, pages 76, 77.

"With the solemn conviction that such momentous events were predicted in the Scriptures to be fulfilled in so short a space of time, the question came home to me with mighty power regarding my duty to the world, in view of the evidence that had affected my own mind."—*Ibid.,* page 81. He could not but feel that it was his duty to impart to others the light which he had received. He expected to encounter opposition from the ungodly, but was confident that all Christians would rejoice in the hope of meeting the Saviour whom they professed to love. His only fear was that in their great joy at the prospect of glorious deliverance, so soon to be consummated, many would receive the doctrine without sufficiently examining the Scriptures in demonstration of its truth. He therefore hesitated to present it, lest he should be in error and be the means of misleading others. He was thus led to review the evidences in support of the conclusions at which he had arrived, and to consider carefully every difficulty which presented itself to his mind. He found that objections vanished before the light of God's word, as mist before the rays of the sun. Five years spent thus left him fully convinced of the correctness of his position.

And now the duty of making known to others what he believed to be so clearly taught in the Scriptures, urged itself with new force upon him. "When I was about my business," he said, "it was continually ringing in my ears, 'Go and tell the world of their danger.' This text was constantly occurring to me: 'When I say unto the wicked, O wicked man, thou shalt surely die; if thou dost not speak to warn the wicked from his way, that wicked man shall die in his iniquity; but his blood will I require at thine hand. Nevertheless, if thou warn the wicked of his way to turn from it; if he do not turn from his way, he shall die in his iniquity; but thou hast delivered thy soul.' Ezekiel 33:8, 9. I felt that if the wicked could be effectually warned, multitudes of them would repent; and that if they were not warned, their blood might be required at my hand."—Bliss, page 92.

He began to present his views in private as he had opportunity, praying that some minister might feel their force and devote himself to their promulgation. But he could not banish the conviction that he had a personal duty to perform in giving the warning. The words were ever recurring to his mind: "Go and tell it to the world; their blood will I require at thy hand." For nine years he waited, the burden still pressing upon his soul, until in 1831 he for the first time publicly gave the reasons of his faith.

As Elisha was called from following his oxen in the field, to receive the mantle of consecration to the prophetic office, so was William Miller called to leave his plow and open to the people the mysteries of the kingdom of God. With trembling he entered upon his work, leading his hearers down, step by step, through the prophetic periods to the second appearing of Christ. With every effort he gained strength and courage as he saw the widespread interest excited by his words.

It was only at the solicitation of his brethren, in whose words he heard the call of God, that Miller consented to present his views in public. He was now fifty years of age, unaccustomed to public speaking, and burdened with a sense of unfitness for the work before him. But from the first his labors were blessed in a remarkable manner to the salvation of souls. His first lecture was followed by a religious awakening in which thirteen entire families, with the exception of two persons, were converted. He was immediately urged to speak in other places, and in nearly every place his labor resulted in a revival of the work of God. Sinners were converted, Christians were roused to greater consecration, and deists and infidels were led to acknowledge the truth of the Bible and the Christian religion. The testimony of those among whom he labored was: "A class of minds are reached by him not within the influence of other men."—*Ibid.*, page 138. His preaching was calculated to arouse the public mind to the great things of religion and to check the growing worldliness and sensuality of the age.

In nearly every town there were scores, in some, hundreds, converted as a result of his preaching. In many places Protestant churches of nearly all denominations were thrown open to him, and the invitations to labor usually came from the ministers of the several congregations. It was his invariable rule not to labor in any place to which he had not been invited, yet he soon found himself unable to comply with half the requests that poured in upon him. Many who did not accept his views as to the exact time of the second advent were convinced of the certainty and nearness of Christ's coming and their need of preparation. In some of the large cities his work produced a marked impression. Liquor dealers abandoned the traffic and turned their shops into meeting rooms; gambling dens were broken up; infidels, deists, Universalists, and even the most abandoned profligates were reformed, some of whom had not entered a house of worship for years. Prayer meetings were established by the various denominations, in different quarters, at almost every hour, businessmen assembling at midday for prayer and praise. There was no extravagant excitement, but an almost universal solemnity on the minds of the people. His work, like that of the early Reformers, tended rather to convince the understanding and arouse the conscience than merely to excite the emotions.

In 1833 Miller received a license to preach, from the Baptist Church, of which he was a member. A large number of the ministers of his denomination also approved his work, and it was with their formal sanction that he continued his labors. He traveled and preached unceasingly, though his personal labors were confined principally to the New England and Middle States. For several years his expenses were met wholly from his own private purse, and he never afterward received enough to meet the expense of travel to the places where he was invited. Thus his public labors, so far from being a pecuniary benefit, were a heavy tax upon his property, which gradually diminished during this period of his life. He was the father of a large family, but as they were all frugal and industrious, his farm sufficed for their maintenance as well as his own.

In 1833, two years after Miller began to present in public the evidences of Christ's soon coming, the last of the signs appeared which were promised by the Saviour as tokens of His second advent. Said Jesus: "The stars shall fall from heaven." Matthew 24:29. And John in the Revelation declared, as he beheld in vision the scenes that should herald the day of God: "The stars of heaven fell unto the earth, even as a fig tree casteth her untimely figs, when she is shaken of a mighty wind." Revelation 6:13. This prophecy received a striking and impressive fulfillment in the great meteoric shower of November 13, 1833. That was the most extensive and wonderful display of falling stars which has ever been recorded; "the whole firmament, over all the United States, being then, for hours, in fiery commotion! No celestial phenomenon has ever occurred in this country, since its first settlement, which was viewed with such intense admiration by one class in the community, or with so much dread and alarm by another." "Its sublimity and awful beauty still linger in many minds. ... Never did rain fall much thicker than the meteors fell toward the earth; east, west, north, and south, it was the same. In a word, the whole heavens seemed in motion. ... The display, as described in Professor Silliman's *Journal*, was seen all over North America. ... From two o'clock until broad daylight, the sky being perfectly serene and cloudless, an incessant play of dazzlingly brilliant luminosities was kept up in the whole heavens."—R. M. Devens, *American Progress; or, The Great Events of the Greatest Century*, ch. 28, pars. 1-5.

"No language, indeed, can come up to the splendor of that magnificent display; ... no one who did not witness it can form an adequate conception of its glory. It seemed as if the whole starry heavens had congregated at one point near the zenith, and were simultaneously shooting forth, with the velocity of lightning, to every part of the horizon; and yet they were not exhausted—thousands swiftly followed in the tracks of thousands, as if created for the occasion."—F. Reed, in the *Christian Advocate and Journal*, Dec. 13, 1833. "A more correct picture of a fig tree casting its figs when blown by a mighty wind, it was not possible to behold."—"The Old Countryman," in Portland *Evening Advertiser*, Nov. 26, 1833.

In the New York *Journal of Commerce* of November 14, 1833, appeared a long article regarding this wonderful phenomenon, containing this state-ment: "No philosopher or scholar has told or recorded an event, I suppose, like that of yesterday morning. A prophet eighteen hundred years ago foretold it exactly, if we will be at the trouble of understanding stars falling to mean falling stars, ... in the only sense in which it is possible to be literally true."

Thus was displayed the last of those signs of His coming, concerning which Jesus bade His disciples: "When ye shall see all these things, *know* that it is near, even at the doors." Matthew 24:33. After these signs, John beheld, as the great event next impending, the heavens departing as a scroll, while the earth quaked, mountains and islands moved out of their places, and the wicked in terror sought to flee from the presence of the Son of man. Revelation 6:12-17.

Many who witnessed the falling of the stars, looked upon it as a herald of the coming judgment, "an awful type, a sure forerunner, a merciful sign, of that great and dreadful day."—"The Old Countryman," in Portland *Evening Advertiser*, Nov. 26, 1833. Thus the attention of the people was directed to the fulfillment of prophecy, and many were led to give heed to the warning of the second advent.

In the year 1840 another remarkable fulfillment of prophecy excited widespread interest. Two years before, Josiah Litch, one of the leading ministers preaching the second advent, published an exposition of Revelation 9, predicting the fall of the Ottoman Empire. According to his calculations, this power was to be overthrown "in A.D. 1840, sometime in the month of August;" and only a few days previous to its accomplishment he wrote: "Allowing the first period, 150 years, to have been exactly fulfilled before Deacozes ascended the throne by permission of the Turks, and that the 391 years, fifteen days, commenced at the close of the first period, it will end on the 11th of August, 1840, when the Ottoman power in Constantinople may be expected to be broken. And this, I believe, will be found to be the case."—Josiah Litch, in *Signs of the Times, and Expositor of Prophecy*, Aug. 1, 1840.

At the very time specified, Turkey, through her ambassadors, accepted the protection of the allied powers of Europe, and thus placed herself under the control of Christian nations. The event exactly fulfilled the prediction. When it became known, multitudes were convinced of the correctness of the principles of prophetic interpretation adopted by Miller and his associates, and a wonderful impetus was given to the advent movement. Men of learning and position united with Miller, both in preaching and in publishing his views, and from 1840 to 1844 the work rapidly extended.

William Miller possessed strong mental powers, disciplined by thought and study; and he added to these the wisdom of heaven by connecting himself with the Source of wisdom. He was a man of sterling worth, who could not but command respect and esteem wherever integrity of character and moral excellence were valued. Uniting true kindness of heart with Christian humility and the power of self-control, he was attentive and affable to all, ready to listen to the opinions of others and to weigh their arguments. Without passion or excitement he tested all theories and doctrines by the word of God, and his sound reasoning and thorough knowledge of the Scriptures enabled him to refute error and expose falsehood.

Yet he did not prosecute his work without bitter opposition. As with earlier Reformers, the truths which he presented were not received with favor by popular religious teachers. As these could not maintain their position by the Scriptures, they were driven to resort to the sayings and doctrines of men, to the traditions of the Fathers. But the word of God was the only testimony accepted by the preachers of the advent truth. "The Bible, and the Bible only," was their watchword. The lack of Scripture argument on the part of their opponents was supplied by ridicule and scoffing. Time, means, and talents were employed in maligning those whose only offense was that they looked with joy for the return of their Lord and were striving to live holy lives and to exhort others to prepare for His appearing.

Earnest were the efforts put forth to draw away the minds of the people from the subject of the second advent. It was made to appear a sin, something of which men should be ashamed, to study the prophecies which relate to the coming of Christ and the end of the world. Thus the popular ministry undermined faith in the word of God. Their teaching made men infidels, and many took license to walk after their own ungodly lusts. Then the authors of the evil charged it all upon Adventists.

While drawing crowded houses of intelligent and attentive hearers, Miller's name was seldom mentioned by the religious press except by way of ridicule or denunciation. The careless and ungodly emboldened by the position of religious teachers, resorted to opprobrious epithets, to base and blasphemous witticisms, in their efforts to heap contumely upon him and his work. The gray-headed man who had left a comfortable home to travel at his own expense from city to city, from town to town, toiling unceasingly to bear to the world the solemn warning of the judgment near, was sneeringly denounced as a fanatic, a liar, a speculating knave.

The ridicule, falsehood, and abuse heaped upon him called forth indignant remonstrance, even from the secular press. "To treat a subject of such overwhelming majesty and fearful consequences," with lightness and ribaldry was declared by worldly men to be "not merely to sport with the feelings of its propagators and advocates," but "to make a jest of the day of judgment, to scoff at the Deity Himself, and contemn the terrors of His judgment bar."—Bliss, page 183.

The instigator of all evil sought not only to counteract the effect of the advent message, but to destroy the messenger himself. Miller made a practical application of Scripture truth to the hearts of his hearers, reproving their sins and disturbing their self-satisfaction, and his plain and cutting words aroused their enmity. The opposition manifested by church members toward his message emboldened the baser classes to go to greater lengths; and enemies plotted to take his life as he should leave the place of meeting. But holy angels were in the throng, and one of these, in the form of a man, took the arm of this servant of the Lord and led him in safety from the angry mob. His work was not yet done, and Satan and his emissaries were disappointed in their purpose.

Despite all opposition, the interest in the advent movement had continued to increase. From scores and hundreds, the congregations had grown to as many thousands. Large accessions had been made to the various churches, but after a time the spirit of opposition was manifested even against these converts, and the churches began to take disciplinary steps with those who had embraced Miller's views. This action called forth a response from his pen, in an address to Christians of all denominations, urging that if his doctrines were false, he should be shown his error from the Scriptures.

"What have we believed," he said, "that we have not been commanded to believe by the word of God, which you yourselves allow is the rule, and only rule, of our faith and practice? What have we done that should call down such virulent denunciations against us from pulpit and press, and give you just cause to exclude us [Adventists] from your churches and fellowship?" "If we are wrong, pray show us wherein consists our wrong. Show us from the word of God that we are in error; we have had ridicule enough; that can never convince us that we are in the wrong; the word of God alone can change our views. Our conclusions have been formed deliberately and prayerfully, as we have seen the evidence in the Scriptures."—*Ibid.,* pages 250, 252.

From age to age the warnings which God has sent to the world by His servants have been received with like incredulity and unbelief. When the iniquity of the antediluvians moved Him to bring a flood of waters upon the earth, He first made known to them His purpose, that they might have opportunity to turn from their evil ways. For a hundred and twenty years was sounded in their ears the warning to repent, lest the wrath of God be manifested in their destruction. But the message seemed to them an idle tale, and they believed it not. Emboldened in their wickedness they mocked the messenger of God, made light of his entreaties, and even accused him of presumption. How dare one man stand up against all the great men of the earth? If Noah's message were true, why did not all the world see it and believe it? One man's assertion against the wisdom of thousands! They would not credit the warning, nor would they seek shelter in the ark.

Scoffers pointed to the things of nature,—to the unvarying succession of the seasons, to the blue skies that had never poured out rain, to the green fields refreshed by the soft dews of night,—and they cried out: "Doth he not speak parables?" In contempt they declared the preacher of righteousness to be a wild enthusiast; and they went on, more eager in their pursuit of pleasure, more intent upon their evil ways, than before. But their unbelief did not hinder the predicted event. God bore long with their wickedness, giving them ample opportunity for repentance; but at the appointed time His judgments were visited upon the rejecters of His mercy.

Christ declares that there will exist similar unbelief concerning His second coming. As the people of Noah's day "knew not until the Flood came, and took them all away; so," in the words of our Saviour, "shall also the coming of the Son of man be." Matthew 24-39. When the professed people of God are uniting with the world, living as they live, and joining with them in forbidden pleasures; when the luxury of the world becomes the luxury of the church; when the marriage bells are chiming, and all are looking forward to many years of worldly prosperity—then, suddenly as the lightning flashes from the heavens, will come the end of their bright visions and delusive hopes.

As God sent His servant to warn the world of the coming Flood, so He sent chosen messengers to make known the nearness of the final judgment. And as Noah's contemporaries laughed to scorn the predictions of the preacher of righteousness, so in Miller's day many, even of the professed people of God, scoffed at the words of warning.

And why were the doctrine and preaching of Christ's second coming so unwelcome to the churches? While to the wicked the advent of the Lord brings woe and desolation, to the righteous it is fraught with joy and hope. This great truth had been the consolation of God's faithful ones through all the ages; why had it become, like its Author, "a stone of stumbling" and "a rock of offense" to His professed people? It was our Lord Himself who promised His disciples: "If I go and prepare a place for you, I will come again, and receive you unto Myself." John 14:3. It was the compassionate Saviour, who, anticipating the loneliness and sorrow of His followers, commissioned angels to comfort them with the assurance that He would come again in person, even as He went into heaven. As the disciples stood gazing intently upward to catch the last glimpse of Him whom they loved, their attention was arrested by the words: "Ye men of Galilee, why stand ye gazing up into heaven? this same Jesus, which is taken up from you into heaven, shall so come in like manner as ye have seen Him go into heaven." Acts 1:11. Hope was kindled afresh by the angels' message. The disciples "returned to Jerusalem with great joy: and were continually in the temple, praising and blessing God." Luke 24:52, 53. They were not rejoicing because Jesus had been separated from them and they were left to struggle with the trials and temptations of the world, but because of the angels' assurance that He would come again.

The proclamation of Christ's coming should now be, as when made by the angels to the shepherds of Bethlehem, good tidings of great joy. Those who really love the Saviour cannot but hail with gladness the announcement founded upon the word of God that He in whom their hopes of eternal life are centered is coming again, not to be insulted, despised, and rejected, as at His first advent, but in power and glory, to redeem His people. It is those who do not love the Saviour that desire Him to remain away, and there can be no more conclusive evidence that the churches have departed from God than the irritation and animosity excited by this Heaven-sent message.

Those who accepted the advent doctrine were roused to the necessity of repentance and humiliation before God. Many had long been halting between Christ and the world; now they felt that it was time to take a stand. "The things of eternity assumed to them an unwonted reality. Heaven was brought near, and they felt themselves guilty before God."—Bliss, page 146. Christians were quickened to new spiritual life. They were made to feel that time was short, that what they had to do for their fellow men must be done quickly. Earth receded, eternity seemed to open before them, and the soul, with all that pertained to its immortal weal or woe, was felt to eclipse every temporal object. The Spirit of God rested upon them and gave power to their earnest appeals to their brethren, as well as to sinners, to prepare for the day of God. The silent testimony of their daily life was a constant rebuke to formal and unconsecrated church members. These did not wish to be disturbed in their pursuit of pleasure, their devotion to money-making, and their ambition for worldly honor. Hence the enmity and opposition excited against the advent faith and those who proclaimed it.

As the arguments from the prophetic periods were found to be impregnable, opposers endeavored to discourage investigation of the subject by teaching that the prophecies were sealed. Thus Protestants followed in the steps of Romanists. While the papal church withholds the Bible from the people, Protestant churches claimed that an important part of the Sacred Word—and that the part which brings to view truths specially applicable to our time—could not be understood.

Ministers and people declared that the prophecies of Daniel and the Revelation were incomprehensible mysteries. But Christ directed His disciples to the words of the prophet Daniel concerning events to take place in their time, and said: "Whoso readeth, let him *understand*." Matthew 24:15. And the assertion that the Revelation is a mystery, not to be understood, is contradicted by the very title of the book: "The Revelation of Jesus Christ, which God gave unto Him, to show unto His servants things which must shortly come to pass. ... *Blessed* is he that *readeth*, and they that *hear* the words of this prophecy, and *keep* those things which are written therein: for the time is at hand." Revelation 1:1-3.

Says the prophet: "Blessed is he that readeth"—there are those who will not read; the blessing is not for them. "And they that hear"—there are some, also, who refuse to hear anything concerning the prophecies; the blessing is not for this class. "And keep those things which are written therein"— many refuse to heed the warnings and instructions contained in the Revelation; none of these can claim the blessing promised. All who ridicule the subjects of the prophecy and mock at the symbols here solemnly given, all who refuse to reform their lives and to prepare for the coming of the Son of man, will be unblessed.

In view of the testimony of Inspiration, how dare men teach that the Revelation is a mystery beyond the reach of human understanding? It is a mystery revealed, a book opened. The study of the Revelation directs the mind to the prophecies of Daniel, and both present most important instruction, given of God to men, concerning events to take place at the close of this world's history.

To John were opened scenes of deep and thrilling interest in the experience of the church. He saw the position, dangers, conflicts, and final deliverance of the people of God. He records the closing messages which are to ripen the harvest of the earth, either as sheaves for the heavenly garner or as fagots for the fires of destruction. Subjects of vast importance were revealed to him, especially for the last church, that those who should turn from error to truth might be instructed concerning the perils and conflicts before them. None need be in darkness in regard to what is coming upon the earth.

Why, then, this widespread ignorance concerning an important part of Holy Writ? Why this general reluctance to investigate its teachings? It is the result of a studied effort of the prince of darkness to conceal from men that which reveals his deceptions. For this reason, Christ the Revelator, foreseeing the warfare that would be waged against the study of the Revelation, pronounced a blessing upon all who should read, hear, and observe the words of the prophecy.

Four

—Light Through Darkness—

Т he work of God in the earth presents, from age to age, a striking similarity in every great reformation or religious movement. The principles of God's dealing with men are ever the same. The important movements of the present have their parallel in those of the past, and the experience of the church in former ages has lessons of great value for our own time.

No truth is more clearly taught in the Bible than that God by His Holy Spirit especially directs His servants on earth in the great movements for the carrying forward of the work of salvation. Men are instruments in the hand of God, employed by Him to accomplish His purposes of grace and mercy. Each has his part to act; to each is granted a measure of light, adapted to the necessities of his time, and sufficient to enable him to perform the work which God has given him to do. But no man, however honored of Heaven, has ever attained to a full understanding of the great plan of redemption, or even to a perfect appreciation of the divine purpose in the work for his own time. Men do not fully understand what God would accomplish by the work which He gives them to do; they do not comprehend, in all its bearings, the message which they utter in His name.

"Canst thou by searching find out God? canst thou find out the Almighty unto perfection?" "My thoughts are not your thoughts, neither are your ways My ways, saith the Lord. For as the heavens are higher than the earth, so are My ways higher than your ways, and My thoughts than your thoughts." "I am God, and there is none like Me, declaring the end from the beginning, and from ancient times the things that are not yet done." Job 11:7; Isaiah 55:8, 9; 46:9, 10.

Even the prophets who were favored with the special illumination of the Spirit did not fully comprehend the import of the revelations committed to them. The meaning was to be unfolded from age to age, as the people of God should need the instruction therein contained.

Peter, writing of the salvation brought to light through the gospel, says: Of this salvation "the prophets have inquired and searched diligently, who prophesied of the grace that should come unto you: searching *what*, or *what manner of time* the Spirit of Christ which was in them did signify, when it testified beforehand the sufferings of Christ, and the glory that should follow. Unto whom it was revealed, that not unto *themselves*, but unto *us* they did minister." 1 Peter 1:10-12.

Yet while it was not given to the prophets to understand fully the things revealed to them, they earnestly sought to obtain all the light which God had been pleased to make manifest. They "inquired and searched diligently," "searching what, or what manner of time the Spirit of Christ which was in them did signify." What a lesson to the people of God in the Christian age, for whose benefit these prophecies were given to His servants! "Unto whom it was revealed, that not unto themselves, but unto us they did minister." Witness those holy men of God as they "inquired and searched diligently" concerning revelations given them for generations that were yet unborn. Contrast their holy zeal with the listless unconcern with which the favored ones of later ages treat this gift of Heaven. What a rebuke to the ease-loving, world-loving indifference which is content to declare that the prophecies cannot be understood!

Though the finite minds of men are inadequate to enter into the counsels of the Infinite One, or to understand fully the working out of His purposes, yet often it is because of some error or neglect on their own part that they so dimly comprehend the messages of Heaven. Not infrequently the minds of the people, and even of God's servants, are so blinded by human opinions, the traditions and false teaching of men, that they are able only partially to grasp the great things which He has revealed in His word. Thus it was with the disciples of Christ, even when the Saviour was with them in person. Their minds had become imbued with the popular conception of the Messiah as a temporal prince, who was to exalt Israel to the throne of the universal empire, and they could not understand the meaning of His words foretelling His sufferings and death.

Christ Himself had sent them forth with the message: "The time is fulfilled, and the kingdom of God is at hand: repent ye, and believe the gospel." Mark 1:15. That message was based on the prophecy of Daniel

9. The sixty-nine weeks were declared by the angel to extend to "the Messiah the Prince," and with high hopes and joyful anticipations the disciples looked forward to the establishment of Messiah's kingdom at Jerusalem to rule over the whole earth.

They preached the message which Christ had committed to them, though they themselves misapprehended its meaning. While their announcement was founded on Daniel 9:25, they did not see, in the next verse of the same chapter, that Messiah was to be cut off. From their very birth their hearts had been set upon the anticipated glory of an earthly empire, and this blinded their understanding alike to the specifications of the prophecy and to the words of Christ.

They performed their duty in presenting to the Jewish nation the invitation of mercy, and then, at the very time when they expected to see their Lord ascend the throne of David, they beheld Him seized as a malefactor, scourged, derided, and condemned, and lifted up on the cross of Calvary. What despair and anguish wrung the hearts of those disciples during the days while their Lord was sleeping in the tomb!

Christ had come at the exact time and in the manner foretold by prophecy. The testimony of Scripture had been fulfilled in every detail of His ministry. He had preached the message of salvation, and "His word was with power." The hearts of His hearers had witnessed that it was of Heaven. The word and the Spirit of God attested the divine commission of His Son.

The disciples still clung with undying affection to their beloved Master. And yet their minds were shrouded in uncertainty and doubt. In their anguish they did not then recall the words of Christ pointing forward to His suffering and death. If Jesus of Nazareth had been the true Messiah, would they have been thus plunged in grief and disappointment? This was the question that tortured their souls while the Saviour lay in His sepulcher during the hopeless hours of that Sabbath which intervened between His death and His resurrection.

Though the night of sorrow gathered dark about these followers of Jesus, yet were they not forsaken. Saith the prophet: "When I sit in darkness, the Lord shall be a light unto me. ... He will bring me forth to the light, and I shall behold His righteousness." "Yea, the darkness hideth not from Thee; but the night shineth as the day: the darkness and the light are both alike to Thee." God hath spoken: "Unto the upright there ariseth light in the darkness." "I will bring the blind by a way that they knew not; I will lead them in paths that they have not known:

I will make darkness light before them, and crooked things straight. These things will I do unto them, and not forsake them." Micah 7:8, 9; Psalms 139:12; 112:4; Isaiah 42:16.

The announcement which had been made by the disciples in the name of the Lord was in every particular correct, and the events to which it pointed were even then taking place. "The time is fulfilled, the kingdom of God is at hand," had been their message. At the expiration of "the time"—the sixty-nine weeks of Daniel 9, which were to extend to the Messiah, "the Anointed One"—Christ had received the anointing of the Spirit after His baptism by John in Jordan. And the "kingdom of God" which they had declared to be at hand was established by the death of Christ. This kingdom was not, as they had been taught to believe, an earthly empire. Nor was it that future, immortal kingdom which shall be set up when "the kingdom and dominion, and the greatness of the kingdom under the whole heaven, shall be given to the people of the saints of the Most High;" that everlasting kingdom, in which "all dominions shall serve and obey Him." Daniel 7:27. As used in the Bible, the expression "kingdom of God" is employed to designate both the kingdom of grace and the kingdom of glory. The kingdom of grace is brought to view by Paul in the Epistle to the Hebrews. After pointing to Christ, the compassionate intercessor who is "touched with the feeling of our infirmities," the apostle says: "Let us therefore come boldly unto *the throne of grace*, that we may obtain mercy, and find grace." Hebrews 4:15, 16. The throne of grace represents the kingdom of grace; for the existence of a throne implies the existence of a kingdom. In many of His parables Christ uses the expression "the kingdom of heaven" to designate the work of divine grace upon the hearts of men.

So the throne of glory represents the kingdom of glory; and this kingdom is referred to in the Saviour's words: "When the Son of man shall come in His glory, and all the holy angels with Him, then shall He sit upon the throne of His glory: and before Him shall be gathered all nations." Matthew 25:31, 32. This kingdom is yet future. It is not to be set up until the second advent of Christ.

The kingdom of grace was instituted immediately after the fall of man, when a plan was devised for the redemption of the guilty race. It then existed in the purpose and by the promise of God; and through faith, men could become its subjects. Yet it was not actually established until the death of Christ. Even after entering upon His earthly mission, the Saviour, wearied with the stubbornness and ingratitude of men, might have drawn back from the sacrifice of Calvary. In Gethsemane the cup of woe trembled in His hand. He might even then have wiped the blood-sweat from His brow and have left the guilty race to perish in their iniquity. Had He done this, there could have been no redemption for fallen men. But when the Saviour yielded up His life, and with His expiring breath cried out, "It is finished," then the fulfillment of the plan of redemption was assured. The promise of salvation made to the sinful pair in Eden was ratified. The kingdom of grace, which had before existed by the promise of God, was then established.

Thus the death of Christ—the very event which the disciples had looked upon as the final destruction of their hope —was that which made it forever sure. While it had brought them a cruel disappointment, it was the climax of proof that their belief had been correct. The event that had filled them with mourning and despair was that which opened the door of hope to every child of Adam, and in which centered the future life and eternal happiness of all God's faithful ones in all the ages.

Purposes of infinite mercy were reaching their fulfillment, even through the disappointment of the disciples. While their hearts had been won by the divine grace and power of His teaching, who "spake as never man spake," yet intermingled with the pure gold of their love for Jesus, was the base alloy of worldly pride and selfish ambitions. Even in the Passover chamber, at that solemn hour when their Master was already entering the shadow of Gethsemane, there was "a strife among them, which of them should be accounted the greatest." Luke 22:24. Their vision was filled with the throne, the crown, and the glory, while just before them lay the shame and agony of the garden, the judgment hall, the cross of Calvary. It was their pride of heart, their thirst for worldly glory, that had led them to cling so tenaciously to the false teaching of their time, and to pass unheeded the Saviour's words showing the true nature of His kingdom, and pointing forward to His agony and death. And these errors resulted in the trial—sharp but needful—which was permitted for their correction. Though the disciples had mistaken the meaning of their message, and had failed to realize their expectations, yet they had preached the warning given them of God, and the Lord would reward their faith and honor their obedience. To them was to be entrusted the work of heralding to all nations the glorious gospel of their risen Lord. It was to prepare them for this work that the experience which seemed to them so bitter had been permitted.

After His resurrection Jesus appeared to His disciples on the way to Emmaus, and, "beginning at Moses and all the prophets, He expounded unto them in all the Scriptures the things concerning Himself." Luke 24:27. The hearts of the disciples were stirred. Faith was kindled. They were "begotten again into a lively hope" even before Jesus revealed Himself to them. It was His purpose to enlighten their understanding and to fasten their faith upon the "sure word of prophecy." He wished the truth to take firm root in their minds, not merely because it was supported by His personal testimony, but because of the unquestionable evidence presented by the symbols and shadows of the typical law, and by the prophecies of the Old Testament. It was needful for the followers of Christ to have an intelligent faith, not only in their own behalf, but that they might carry the knowledge of Christ to the world. And as the very first step in imparting this knowledge, Jesus directed the disciples to "Moses and all the prophets." Such was the testimony given by the risen Saviour to the value and importance of the Old Testament Scriptures.

What a change was wrought in the hearts of the disciples as they looked once more on the loved countenance of their Master! Luke 24:32. In a more complete and perfect sense than ever before they had "found Him, of whom Moses in the law, and the prophets, did write." The uncertainty, the anguish, the despair, gave place to perfect assurance, to unclouded faith. What marvel that after His ascension they "were continually in the temple, praising and blessing God." The people, knowing only of the Saviour's ignominious death, looked to see in their faces the expression of sorrow, confusion, and defeat; but they saw there gladness and triumph. What a preparation these disciples had received for the work before them! They had passed through the deepest trial which it was possible for them to experience, and had seen how, when to human vision all was lost, the word of God had been triumphantly accomplished. Henceforward what could daunt their faith or chill the ardor of their love? In the keenest sorrow they had "strong consolation," a hope which was as "an anchor of the soul, both sure and steadfast." Hebrews 6:18, 19. They had been witness to the wisdom and power of God, and they were "persuaded, that neither death, nor life, nor angels, nor principalities, nor powers, nor things present, nor things to come, nor height, nor depth, nor any other creature," would be able to separate them from "the love of God, which is in Christ Jesus our Lord." "In all these things," they said, "we are more than conquerors through Him that loved us." Romans 8:38, 39, 37. "The word of the Lord endureth forever." 1 Peter 1:25. And "who is he that condemneth? It is Christ that died, yea rather, that is *risen again*, who is even at the right hand of God, who also maketh intercession for us." Romans 8:34.

Saith the Lord: "My people shall never be ashamed." Joel 2:26. "Weeping may endure for a night, but joy cometh in the morning." Psalm 30:5. When on His resurrection day these disciples met the Saviour, and their hearts burned within them as they listened to His words; when they looked upon the head and hands and feet that had been bruised for them; when, before His ascension, Jesus led them out as far as Bethany, and lifting up His hands in blessing, bade them, "Go ye into all the world, and preach the gospel," adding, "Lo, I am with you alway" (Mark 16:15; Matthew 28:20); when on the Day of Pentecost the promised Comforter descended and the power from on high was given and the souls of the believers thrilled with the conscious presence of their ascended Lord—then, even though, like His, their pathway led through sacrifice and martyrdom, would they have exchanged the ministry of the gospel of His grace, with the "crown of righteousness" to be received at His coming, for the glory of an earthly throne, which had been the hope of their earlier discipleship? He who is "able to do exceeding abundantly above all that we ask or think," had granted them, with the fellowship of His sufferings, the communion of His joy—the joy of "bringing many sons unto glory," joy unspeakable, an "eternal weight of glory," to which, says Paul, "our light affliction, which is but for a moment," is "not worthy to be compared."

The experience of the disciples who preached the "gospel of the kingdom" at the first advent of Christ, had its counterpart in the experience of those who proclaimed the message of His second advent. As the disciples went out preaching, "The time is fulfilled, the kingdom of God is at hand," so Miller and his associates proclaimed that the longest and last prophetic period brought to view in the Bible was about to expire, that the judgment was at hand, and the everlasting kingdom was to be ushered in. The preaching of the disciples in regard to time was based on the seventy weeks of Daniel 9. The message given by Miller and his associates announced the termination of the 2,300 days of Daniel 8:14, of which the seventy weeks form a part. The preaching of each was based upon the fulfillment of a different portion of the same great prophetic period.

Like the first disciples, William Miller and his associates did not, themselves, fully comprehend the import of the message which they bore. Errors that had been long established in the church prevented them from arriving at a correct interpretation of an important point in the prophecy. Therefore, though they proclaimed the message which God had committed to them to be given to the world, yet through a misapprehension of its meaning they suffered disappointment.

In explaining Daniel 8:14, "Unto two thousand and three hundred days; then shall the sanctuary be cleansed," Miller, as has been stated, adopted the generally received view that the earth is the sanctuary, and he believed that the cleansing of the sanctuary represented the purification of the earth by fire at the coming of the Lord. When, therefore, he found that the close of the 2,300 days was definitely foretold, he concluded that this revealed the time of the second advent. His error resulted from accepting the popular view as to what constitutes the sanctuary.

In the typical system, which was a shadow of the sacrifice and priesthood of Christ, the cleansing of the sanctuary was the last service performed by the high priest in the yearly round of ministration. It was the closing work of the atonement—a removal or putting away of sin from Israel. It prefigured the closing work in the ministration of our High Priest in heaven, in the removal or blotting out of the sins of His people, which are registered in the heavenly records. This service involves a work of investigation, a work of judgment; and it immediately precedes the coming of Christ in the clouds of heaven with power and great glory; for when He comes, every case has been decided. Says Jesus: "My reward is with Me, to give every man according as his work shall be." Revelation 22:12. It is this work of judgment, immediately preceding the second advent, that is announced in the first angel's message of Revelation 4:7: "Fear God, and give glory to Him; for the hour of His judgment is come."

Those who proclaimed this warning gave the right message at the right time. But as the early disciples declared, "The time is fulfilled, and the kingdom of God is at hand," based on the prophecy of Daniel 9, while they failed to perceive that the death of the Messiah was foretold in the same scripture, so Miller and his associates preached the message based on Daniel 8:14 and Revelation 14:7, and failed to see that there were still other messages brought to view in Revelation 14, which were also to be given before the advent of the Lord. As the disciples were mistaken in regard to the kingdom to be set up at the end of the seventy weeks, so Adventists were mistaken in regard to the event to take place at the expiration of the 2,300 days. In both cases there was an acceptance of, or rather an adherence to, popular errors that blinded the mind to the truth. Both classes fulfilled the will of God in delivering the message which He desired to be given, and both, through their own misapprehension of their message, suffered disappointment.

Yet God accomplished His own beneficent purpose in permitting the warning of the judgment to be given just as it was. The great day was at hand, and in His providence the people were brought to the test of a definite time, in order to reveal to them what was in their hearts. The message was designed for the testing and purification of the church. They were to be led to see whether their affections were set upon this world or upon Christ and heaven. They professed to love the Saviour; now they were to prove their love. Were they ready to renounce their worldly hopes and ambitions, and welcome with joy the advent of their Lord? The message was designed to enable them to discern their true spiritual state; it was sent in mercy to arouse them to seek the Lord with repentance and humiliation.

The disappointment also, though the result of their own misapprehension of the message which they gave, was to be overruled for good. It would test the hearts of those who had professed to receive the warning. In the face of their disappointment would they rashly give up their experience and cast away their confidence in God's word? or would they, in prayer and humility, seek to discern where they had failed to comprehend the significance of the prophecy? How many had moved from fear, or from impulse and excitement? How many were halfhearted and unbelieving? Multitudes professed to love the appearing of the Lord. When called to endure the scoffs and reproach of the world, and the test of delay and disappointment, would they renounce the faith? Because they did not immediately understand the dealings of God with them, would they cast aside truths sustained by the clearest testimony of His word?

This test would reveal the strength of those who with real faith had obeyed what they believed to be the teaching of the word and the Spirit of God. It would teach them, as only such an experience could, the danger of accepting the theories and interpretations of men, instead of making the Bible its own interpreter. To the children of faith the perplexity and sorrow resulting from their error would work the needed correction. They would be led to a closer study of the prophetic word. They would be taught to examine more carefully the foundation of their faith, and to reject everything, however widely accepted by the Christian world, that was not founded upon the Scriptures of truth.

With these believers, as with the first disciples, that which in the hour of trial seemed dark to their understanding would afterward be made plain. When they should see the "end of the Lord" they would know that, notwithstanding the trial resulting from their errors, His purposes of love toward them had been steadily fulfilling. They would learn by a blessed experience that He is "very pitiful, and of tender mercy;" that all His paths "are mercy and truth unto such as keep His covenant and His testimonies."

Five

—A Great Religious Awakening—

A great religious awakening under the proclamation of Christ's soon coming is foretold in the prophecy of the first angel's message of Revelation 14. An angel is seen flying "in the midst of heaven, having the everlasting gospel to preach unto them that dwell on the earth, and to every nation, and kindred, and tongue, and people." "With a loud voice" he proclaims the message: "Fear God, and give glory to Him; for the hour of His judgment is come: and worship Him that made heaven, and earth, and the sea, and the fountains of waters." Verses 6, 7.

The fact that an angel is said to be the herald of this warning is significant. By the purity, the glory, and the power of the heavenly messenger, divine wisdom has been pleased to represent the exalted character of the work to be accomplished by the message and the power and glory that were to attend it. And the angel's flight "in the midst of heaven," the "loud voice" with which the warning is uttered, and its promulgation to all "that dwell on the earth,"—"to every nation, and kindred, and tongue, and people,"—give evidence of the rapidity and worldwide extent of the movement.

The message itself sheds light as to the time when this movement is to take place. It is declared to be a part of the "everlasting gospel;" and it announces the opening of the judgment. The message of salvation has been preached in all ages; but this message is a part of the gospel which could be proclaimed only in the last days, for only then would it be true that the hour of judgment *had come*. The prophecies present a succession of events leading down to the opening of the judgment. This is especially true of the book of Daniel. But that part of his prophecy which related to the last days, Daniel was bidden to close up and seal "to the time of the end." Not till we reach this time could a message concerning the judgment be proclaimed, based on the fulfillment of these prophecies. But at the time of the end, says the prophet, "many shall run to and fro, and knowledge shall be increased." Daniel 12:4.

The apostle Paul warned the church not to look for the coming of Christ in his day. "That day shall not come," he says, "except there come a falling away first, and that man of sin be revealed." 2 Thessalonians 2:3. Not till after the great apostasy, and the long period of the reign of the "man of sin," can we look for the advent of our Lord. The "man of sin," which is also styled "the mystery of iniquity," "the son of perdition," and "that wicked," represents the papacy, which, as foretold in prophecy, was to maintain its supremacy for 1260 years. This period ended in 1798. The coming of Christ could not take place before that time. Paul covers with his caution the whole of the Christian dispensation down to the year 1798. It is this side of that time that the message of Christ's second coming is to be proclaimed.

No such message has ever been given in past ages. Paul, as we have seen, did not preach it; he pointed his brethren into the then far-distant future for the coming of the Lord. The Reformers did not proclaim it. Martin Luther placed the judgment about three hundred years in the future from his day. But since 1798 the book of Daniel has been unsealed, knowledge of the prophecies has increased, and many have proclaimed the solemn message of the judgment near.

Like the great Reformation of the sixteenth century, the advent movement appeared in different countries of Christendom at the same time. In both Europe and America men of faith and prayer were led to the study of the prophecies, and, tracing down the inspired record, they saw convincing evidence that the end of all things was at hand. In different lands there were isolated bodies of Christians who, solely by the study of the Scriptures, arrived at the belief that the Saviour's advent was near.

In 1821, three years after Miller had arrived at his exposition of the prophecies pointing to the time of the judgment, Dr. Joseph Wolff, "the missionary to the world," began to proclaim the Lord's soon coming. Wolff was born in Germany, of Hebrew parentage, his father being a Jewish rabbi. While very young he was convinced of the truth of the Christian religion. Of an active, inquiring mind, he had been an eager listener to the conversations that took place in his father's house as devout Hebrews daily assembled to recount the hopes and anticipations of their people, the glory of the coming Messiah, and the restoration of

Israel. One day hearing Jesus of Nazareth mentioned, the boy inquired who He was. "A Jew of the greatest talent," was the answer; "but as He pretended to be the Messiah, the Jewish tribunal sentenced Him to death." "Why," rejoined the questioner, "is Jerusalem destroyed, and why are we in captivity?" "Alas, alas!" answered his father, "because the Jews murdered the prophets." The thought was at once suggested to the child: "Perhaps Jesus was also a prophet, and the Jews killed Him when He was innocent."—*Travels and Adventures of the Rev. Joseph Wolff*, vol. 1, p. 6. So strong was this feeling that, though forbidden to enter a Christian church, he would often linger outside to listen to the preaching.

When only seven years old he was boasting to an aged Christian neighbor of the future triumph of Israel at the advent of the Messiah, when the old man said kindly: "Dear boy, I will tell you who the real Messiah was: He was Jesus of Nazareth, … whom your ancestors have crucified, as they did the prophets of old. Go home and read the fifty-third chapter of Isaiah, and you will be convinced that Jesus Christ is the Son of God."—*Ibid.*, vol. 1, p. 7. Conviction at once fastened upon him. He went home and read the scripture, wondering to see how perfectly it had been fulfilled in Jesus of Nazareth. Were the words of the Christian true? The boy asked of his father an explanation of the prophecy, but was met with a silence so stern that he never again dared to refer to the subject. This, however, only increased his desire to know more of the Christian religion.

The knowledge he sought was studiously kept from him in his Jewish home; but, when only eleven years old, he left his father's house and went out into the world to gain for himself an education, to choose his religion and his lifework. He found a home for a time with kinsmen, but was soon driven from them as an apostate, and alone and penniless he had to make his own way among strangers. He went from place to place, studying diligently and maintaining himself by teaching Hebrew. Through the influence of a Catholic instructor he was led to accept the Romish faith and formed the purpose of becoming a missionary to his own people. With this object he went, a few years later, to pursue his studies in the College of the Propaganda at Rome. Here his habit of independent thought and candid speech brought upon him the imputation of heresy. He openly attacked the abuses of the church and urged the necessity of reform. Though at first treated with special favor by the papal dignitaries, he was after a time removed from Rome. Under the surveillance of the church he went from place to place, until it became evident that he could never be brought to submit to the bondage of Romanism. He was declared to be incorrigible and was left at liberty to go where he pleased. He now made his way to England and, professing the Protestant faith, united with the English Church. After two years' study he set out, in 1821, upon his mission.

While Wolff accepted the great truth of Christ's first advent as "a Man of Sorrows, and acquainted with grief," he saw that the prophecies bring to view with equal clearness His second advent with power and glory. And while he sought to lead his people to Jesus of Nazareth as the Promised One, and to point them to His first coming in humiliation as a sacrifice for the sins of men, he taught them also of His second coming as a king and deliverer.

"Jesus of Nazareth, the true Messiah," he said, "whose hands and feet were pierced, who was brought like a lamb to the slaughter, who was the Man of Sorrows and acquainted with grief, who after the scepter was taken from Judah, and the legislative power from between his feet, came the first time; shall come the second time in the clouds of heaven, and with the trump of the Archangel" (Joseph Wolff, *Researches and Missionary Labors*, page 62) "and shall stand upon the Mount of Olives; and that dominion, once consigned to Adam over the creation, and forfeited by him (Genesis 1:26; 3:17), shall be given to Jesus. He shall be king over all the earth. The groanings and lamentations of the creation shall cease, but songs of praises and thanksgivings shall be heard. ... When Jesus comes in the glory of His Father, with the holy angels, ... the dead believers shall rise first. 1 Thessalonians 4:16; 1 Corinthians 15:32. This is what we Christians call the first resurrection. Then the animal kingdom shall change its nature (Isaiah 11:6-9), and be subdued unto Jesus. Psalm 8. Universal peace shall prevail."—*Journal of the Rev. Joseph Wolff*, pages 378, 379. "The Lord again shall look down upon the earth, and say, 'Behold, it is very good.'"—*Ibid.*, page 294.

Wolff believed the coming of the Lord to be at hand, his interpretation of the prophetic periods placing the great consummation within a very few years of the time pointed out by Miller. To those who urged from the scripture, "Of that day and hour knoweth no man," that men are to know nothing concerning the nearness of the advent, Wolff replied: "Did our Lord say that that day and hour should *never* be known? Did He not give us signs of the times, in order that we may know at least the *approach* of His coming, as one knows the approach of the summer by the fig tree putting forth its leaves? Matthew 24:32. Are we never to know that period, whilst He Himself exhorteth us not only to read Daniel the prophet, but to understand it? and in that very Daniel, where it is said that the words were shut up to the time of the end (which was the case in his time), and that 'many shall run to and fro' (a Hebrew expression for observing and thinking upon the time), 'and *knowledge*' (regarding that time) 'shall be increased.' Daniel 12:4. Besides this, our Lord does not intend to say by this, that the *approach* of the time shall not be known, but that the *exact 'day* and *hour* knoweth no man.' Enough, He does say, shall be known by the signs of the times, to induce us to prepare for His coming, as Noah prepared the ark."—Wolff, *Researches and Missionary Labors*, pages 404, 405.

Concerning the popular system of interpreting, or misinterpreting, the Scriptures, Wolff wrote: "The greater part of the Christian church have swerved from the plain sense of Scripture, and have turned to the phantomizing system of the Buddhists, who believe that the future happiness of mankind will consist in moving about in the air, and suppose that when they are reading *Jews* they must understand *Gentiles*; and when they read *Jerusalem*, they must understand the *church*; and if it is said *earth*, it means *sky*; and for the coming of the *Lord* they must understand the progress of the *missionary societies*; and going up to the mountain of the Lord's house, signifies a grand *class meeting of Methodists*."—*Journal of the Rev. Joseph Wolff*, page 96.

During the twenty-four years from 1821 to 1845, Wolff traveled extensively: in Africa, visiting Egypt and Abyssinia; in Asia, traversing Palestine, Syria, Persia, Bokhara, and India. He also visited the United States, on the journey thither preaching on the island of Saint Helena. He arrived in New York in August, 1837; and, after speaking in that city, he preached in Philadelphia and Baltimore, and finally proceeded to Washington. Here, he says, "on a motion brought forward by the ex-President, John Quincy Adams, in one of the houses of Congress, the House unanimously granted to me the use of the Congress Hall for a lecture, which I delivered on a Saturday, honored with the presence of all the members of Congress, and also of the bishop of Virginia, and of the clergy and citizens of Washington. The same honor was granted to me by the members of the government of New Jersey and Pennsylvania, in whose presence I delivered lectures on my researches in Asia, and also on the personal reign of Jesus Christ."—*Ibid.,* pages 398, 399.

Dr. Wolff traveled in the most barbarous countries without the protection of any European authority, enduring many hardships and surrounded with countless perils. He was bastinadoed and starved, sold as a slave, and three times condemned to death. He was beset by robbers, and sometimes nearly perished from thirst. Once he was stripped of all that he possessed and left to travel hundreds of miles on foot through the mountains, the snow beating in his face and his naked feet benumbed by contact with the frozen ground.

When warned against going unarmed among savage and hostile tribes, he declared himself "provided with arms"—"prayer, zeal for Christ, and confidence in His help." "I am also," he said, "provided with the love of God and my neighbor in my heart, and the Bible is in my hand."—W.H.D. Adams, *In Perils Oft*, page 192. The Bible in Hebrew and English he carried with him wherever he went. Of one of his later journeys he says: "I ... kept the Bible open in my hand. I felt my power was in the Book, and that its might would sustain me."—*Ibid.,* page 201.

Thus he persevered in his labors until the message of the judgment had been carried to a large part of the habitable globe. Among Jews, Turks, Parsees, Hindus, and many other nationalities and races he distributed the word of God in these various tongues and everywhere heralded the approaching reign of the Messiah.

In his travels in Bokhara he found the doctrine of the Lord's soon coming held by a remote and isolated people. The Arabs of Yemen, he says, "are in possession of a book called *Seera*, which gives notice of the second coming of Christ and His reign in glory; and they expect great events to take place in the year 1840."—*Journal of the Rev. Joseph Wolff*, page 377. "In Yemen ... I spent six days with the children of Rechab. They drink no wine, plant no vineyard, sow no seed, and live in tents, and remember good old Jonadab, the son of Rechab; and I found in their company children of Israel, of the tribe of Dan, ... who expect, with the children of Rechab, the speedy arrival of the Messiah in the clouds of heaven."—*Ibid.,* page 389.

A similar belief was found by another missionary to exist in Tatary. A Tatar priest put the question to the missionary as to when Christ would come the second time. When the missionary answered that he knew nothing about it, the priest seemed greatly surprised at such ignorance in one who professed to be a Bible teacher, and stated his own belief, founded on prophecy, that Christ would come about 1844.

As early as 1826 the advent message began to be preached in England. The movement here did not take so definite a form as in America; the exact time of the advent was not so generally taught, but the great truth of Christ's soon coming in power and glory was extensively proclaimed. And this not among the dissenters and nonconformists only. Mourant Brock, an English writer, states that about seven hundred ministers of the Church of England were engaged in preaching "this gospel of the kingdom." The message pointing to 1844 as the time of the Lord's coming was also given in Great Britain. Advent publications from the United States were widely circulated. Books and journals were republished in England. And in 1842 Robert Winter, an Englishman by birth, who had received the advent faith in America, returned to his native country to herald the coming of the Lord. Many united with him in the work, and the message of the judgment was proclaimed in various parts of England.

In South America, in the midst of barbarism and priestcraft, Lacunza, a Spaniard and a Jesuit, found his way to the Scriptures and thus received the truth of Christ's speedy return. Impelled to give the warning, yet desiring to escape the censures of Rome, he published his views under the assumed name of "Rabbi Ben-Ezra," representing himself as a converted Jew. Lacunza lived in the eighteenth century, but it was about 1825 that his book, having found its way to London, was translated into the English language. Its publication served to deepen the interest already awakening in England in the subject of the second advent.

In Germany the doctrine had been taught in the eighteenth century by Bengel, a minister in the Lutheran Church and a celebrated Biblical scholar and critic. Upon completing his education, Bengel had "devoted himself to the study of theology, to which the grave and religious tone of his mind, deepened by his early training and discipline, naturally inclined him. Like other young men of thoughtful character, before and since, he had to struggle with doubts and difficulties of a religious nature, and he alludes, with much feeling, to the 'many arrows which pierced his poor heart, and made his youth hard to bear.' " Becoming a member of the consistory of Wurttemberg, he advocated the cause of religious liberty. "While maintaining the rights and privileges of the church, he was an advocate for all reasonable freedom being accorded to those who felt themselves bound, on grounds of conscience, to withdraw from her communion."—*Encyclopaedia Britannica*, 9th ed., art. "Bengel." The good effects of this policy are still felt in his native province.

It was while preparing a sermon from Revelation 21 for advent Sunday that the light of Christ's second coming broke in upon Bengel's mind. The prophecies of the Revelation unfolded to his understanding as never before. Overwhelmed with a sense of the stupendous importance and surpassing glory of the scenes presented by the prophet, he was forced to turn for a time from the contemplation of the subject. In the pulpit it again presented itself to him with all its vividness and power. From that time he devoted himself to the study of the prophecies, especially those of the Apocalypse, and soon arrived at the belief that they pointed to the coming of Christ as near. The date which he fixed upon as the time of the second advent was within a very few years of that afterward held by Miller.

Bengel's writings have been spread throughout Christendom. His views of prophecy were quite generally received in his own state of Wurttemberg, and to some extent in other parts of Germany. The movement continued after his death, and the advent message was heard in Germany at the same time that it was attracting attention in other lands. At an early date some of the believers went to Russia and there formed colonies, and the faith of Christ's soon coming is still held by the German churches of that country.

The light shone also in France and Switzerland. At Geneva where Farel and Calvin had spread the truth of the Reformation, Gaussen preached the message of the second advent. While a student at school, Gaussen had encountered that spirit of rationalism which pervaded all Europe during the latter part of the eighteenth and the opening of the nineteenth century; and when he entered the ministry he was not only ignorant of true faith, but inclined to skepticism. In his youth he had become interested in the study of prophecy. After reading Rollin's *Ancient History*, his attention was called to the second chapter of Daniel, and he was struck with the wonderful exactness with which the prophecy had been fulfilled, as seen in the historian's record. Here was a testimony to the inspiration of the Scriptures, which served as an anchor to him amid the perils of later years. He could not rest satisfied with the teachings of rationalism, and in studying the Bible and searching for clearer light he was, after a time, led to a positive faith.

As he pursued his investigation of the prophecies he arrived at the belief that the coming of the Lord was at hand. Impressed with the solemnity and importance of this great truth, he desired to bring it before the people; but the popular belief that the prophecies of Daniel are mysteries and cannot be understood was a serious obstacle in his way. He finally determined—as Farel had done before him in evangelizing Geneva—to begin with the children, through whom he hoped to interest the parents.

"I desire this to be understood," he afterward said, speaking of his object in this undertaking, "it is not because of its small importance, but on the contrary because of its great value, that I wished to present it in this familiar form, and that I addressed it to the children. I desired to be heard, and I feared that I would not be if I addressed myself to the grown people first." "I determined therefore to go to the youngest. I gather an audience of children; if the group enlarges, if it is seen that they listen, are pleased, interested, that they understand and explain the subject, I am sure to have a second circle soon, and in their turn, grown people will see that it is worth their while to sit down and study. When this is done, the cause is gained."—L. Gaussen, *Daniel the Prophet*, vol. 2, Preface.

The effort was successful. As he addressed the children, older persons came to listen. The galleries of his church were filled with attentive hearers. Among them were men of rank and learning, and strangers and foreigners visiting Geneva; and thus the message was carried to other parts.

Encouraged by this success, Gaussen published his lessons, with the hope of promoting the study of the prophetic books in the churches of the French-speaking people. "To publish instruction given to the children," says Gaussen, "is to say to adults, who too often neglect such books under the false pretense that they are obscure, 'How can they be obscure, since your children understand them?' " "I had a great desire," he adds, "to render a knowledge of the prophecies popular in our flocks, if possible." "There is no study, indeed, which it seems to me answers the needs of the time better." "It is by this that we are to prepare for the tribulation near at hand, and watch and wait for Jesus Christ."

Though one of the most distinguished and beloved of preachers in the French language, Gaussen was after a time suspended from the ministry, his principal offense being that instead of the church's catechism, a tame and rationalistic manual, almost destitute of positive faith, he had used the Bible in giving instruction to the youth. He afterward became teacher in a theological school, while on Sunday he continued his work as catechist, addressing the children and instructing them in the Scriptures. His works on prophecy also excited much interest. From the professor's chair, through the press, and in his favorite occupation as teacher of children he continued for many years to exert an extensive influence and was instrumental in calling the attention of many to the study of the prophecies which showed that the coming of the Lord was near.

In Scandinavia also the advent message was proclaimed, and a widespread interest was kindled. Many were roused from their careless security to confess and forsake their sins, and seek pardon in the name of Christ. But the clergy of the state church opposed the movement, and through their influence some who preached the message were thrown into prison. In many places where the preachers of the Lord's soon coming were thus silenced, God was pleased to send the message, in a miraculous manner, through little children. As they were under age, the law of the state could not restrain them, and they were permitted to speak unmolested.

The movement was chiefly among the lower class, and it was in the humble dwellings of the laborers that the people assembled to hear the warning. The child-preachers themselves were mostly poor cottagers. Some of them were not more than six or eight years of age; and while their lives testified that they loved the Saviour, and were trying to live in obedience to God's holy requirements, they ordinarily manifested only the intelligence and ability usually seen in children of that age. When standing before the people, however, it was evident that they were moved by an influence beyond their own natural gifts. Tone and manner changed, and with solemn power they gave the warning of the judgment, employing the very words of Scripture: "Fear God, and give glory to Him; for the hour of His judgment is come." They reproved the sins of the people, not only condemning immorality and vice, but rebuking worldliness and backsliding, and warning their hearers to make haste to flee from the wrath to come.

The people heard with trembling. The convicting Spirit of God spoke to their hearts. Many were led to search the Scriptures with new and deeper interest, the intemperate and immoral were reformed, others abandoned their dishonest practices, and a work was done so marked that even ministers of the state church were forced to acknowledge that the hand of God was in the movement.

It was God's will that the tidings of the Saviour's coming should be given in the Scandinavian countries; and when the voices of His servants were silenced, He put His Spirit upon the children, that the work might be accomplished. When Jesus drew near to Jerusalem attended by the rejoicing multitudes that, with shouts of triumph and the waving of palm branches, heralded Him as the Son of David, the jealous Pharisees called upon Him to silence them; but Jesus answered that all this was in fulfillment of prophecy, and if these should hold their peace, the very stones would cry out. The people, intimidated by the threats of the priests and rulers, ceased their joyful proclamation as they entered the gates of Jerusalem; but the children in the temple courts afterward took up the refrain, and, waving their branches of palm, they cried: "Hosanna to the Son of David!" Matthew 21:8-16. When the Pharisees, sorely displeased, said unto Him, "Hearest Thou what these say?" Jesus answered, "Yea; have ye never read, Out of the mouth of babes and sucklings Thou hast perfected praise?" As God wrought through children at the time of Christ's first advent, so He wrought through them in giving the message of His second advent. God's word must be fulfilled, that the proclamation of the Saviour's coming should be given to all peoples, tongues, and nations.

To William Miller and his colaborers it was given to preach the warning in America. This country became the center of the great advent movement. It was here that the prophecy of the first angel's message had its most direct fulfillment. The writings of Miller and his associates were carried to distant lands. Wherever missionaries had penetrated in all the world, were sent the glad tidings of Christ's speedy return. Far and wide spread the message of the everlasting gospel: "Fear God, and give glory to Him; for the hour of His judgment is come."

The testimony of the prophecies which seemed to point to the coming of Christ in the spring of 1844 took deep hold of the minds of the people. As the message went from state to state, there was everywhere awakened widespread interest. Many were convinced that the arguments from the prophetic periods were correct, and, sacrificing their pride of opinion, they joyfully received the truth. Some ministers laid aside their sectarian views and feelings, left their salaries and their churches, and united in proclaiming the coming of Jesus. There were comparatively few ministers, however, who would accept this message; therefore it was largely committed to humble laymen. Farmers left their fields, mechanics their tools, traders their merchandise, professional men their positions; and yet the number of workers was small in comparison with the work to be accomplished. The condition of an ungodly church and a world lying in wickedness, burdened the souls of the true watchmen, and they willingly endured toil, privation, and suffering, that they might call men to repentance unto salvation. Though opposed by Satan, the work went steadily forward, and the advent truth was accepted by many thousands.

Everywhere the searching testimony was heard, warning sinners, both worldlings and church members, to flee from the wrath to come. Like John the Baptist, the forerunner of Christ, the preachers laid the ax at the root of the tree and urged all to bring forth fruit meet for repentance. Their stirring appeals were in marked contrast to the assurances of peace and safety that were heard from popular pulpits; and wherever the message was given, it moved the people. The simple, direct testimony of the Scriptures, set home by the power of the Holy Spirit, brought a weight of conviction which few were able wholly to resist. Professors of religion were roused from their false security. They saw their backslidings, their worldliness and unbelief, their pride and selfishness. Many sought the Lord with repentance and humiliation. The affections that had so long clung to earthly things they now fixed upon heaven. The Spirit of God rested upon them, and with hearts softened and subdued they joined to sound the cry: "Fear God, and give glory to Him; for the hour of His judgment is come."

Sinners inquired with weeping: "What must I do to be saved?" Those whose lives had been marked with dishonesty were anxious to make restitution. All who found peace in Christ longed to see others share the blessing. The hearts of parents were turned to their children, and the hearts of children to their parents. The barriers of pride and reserve were swept away. Heartfelt confessions were made, and the members of the household labored for the salvation of those who were nearest and dearest. Often was heard the sound of earnest intercession. Everywhere were souls in deep anguish pleading with God. Many wrestled all night in prayer for the assurance that their own sins were pardoned, or for the conversion of their relatives or neighbors.

All classes flocked to the Adventist meetings. Rich and poor, high and low, were, from various causes, anxious to hear for themselves the doctrine of the second advent. The Lord held the spirit of opposition in check while His servants explained the reasons of their faith. Sometimes the instrument was feeble; but the Spirit of God gave power to His truth. The presence of holy angels was felt in these assemblies, and many were daily added to the believers. As the evidences of Christ's soon coming were repeated, vast crowds listened in breathless silence to the solemn words. Heaven and earth seemed to approach each other. The power of God was felt upon old and young and middle-aged. Men sought their homes with praises upon their lips, and the glad sound rang out upon the still night air. None who attended those meetings can ever forget those scenes of deepest interest.

The proclamation of a definite time for Christ's coming called forth great opposition from many of all classes, from the minister in the pulpit down to the most reckless, Heaven-daring sinner. The words of prophecy were fulfilled: "There shall come in the last days scoffers, walking after their own lusts, and saying, Where is the promise of His coming? for since the fathers fell asleep, all things continue as they were from the beginning of the creation." 2 Peter 3:3, 4. Many who professed to love the Saviour, declared that they had no opposition to the doctrine of the second advent; they merely objected to the definite time. But God's all-seeing eye read their hearts. They did not wish to hear of Christ's coming to judge the world in righteousness. They had been unfaithful servants, their works would not bear the inspection of the heart-searching God, and they feared to meet their Lord. Like the Jews at the time of Christ's first advent they were not prepared to welcome Jesus. They not only refused to listen to the plain arguments from the Bible, but ridiculed those who were looking for the Lord. Satan and his angels exulted, and flung the taunt in the face of Christ and holy angels that His professed people had so little love for Him that they did not desire His appearing.

"No man knoweth the day nor the hour" was the argument most often brought forward by rejecters of the advent faith. The scripture is: "Of that day and hour knoweth no man, no not the angels of heaven, but My Father only." Matthew 24:36. A clear and harmonious explanation of this text was given by those who were looking for the Lord, and the wrong use made of it by their opponents was clearly shown. The words were spoken by Christ in that memorable conversation with His disciples upon Olivet after He had for the last time departed from the temple. The disciples had asked the question: "What shall be the sign of Thy coming, and of the end of the world?" Jesus gave them signs, and said: "When ye shall see all these things, know that it is near, even at the doors." Verses 3, 33. One saying of the Saviour must not be made to destroy another. Though no man knoweth the *day* nor the *hour* of His coming, we are instructed and required to know when it is near. We are further taught that to disregard His warning, and refuse or neglect to know when His advent is near, will be as fatal for us as it was for those who lived in the days of Noah not to know when the flood was coming. And the parable in the same chapter, contrasting the faithful and the unfaithful servant, and giving the doom of him who said in his heart, "My Lord delayeth His coming," shows in what light Christ will regard and reward those whom He finds watching, and teaching His coming, and those denying it. "Watch therefore," He says. "Blessed is that servant, whom his Lord when He cometh shall find so doing." Verses 42, 46. "If therefore thou shalt not watch, I will come on thee as a thief, and thou shalt not know what hour I will come upon thee." Revelation 3:3.

Paul speaks of a class to whom the Lord's appearing will come unawares. "The day of the Lord so cometh as a thief in the night. For when they shall say, Peace and safety; then sudden destruction cometh upon them, … and they shall not escape." But he adds, to those who have given heed to the Saviour's warning: "Ye, brethren, are not in darkness, that that day should overtake you as a thief. Ye are all the children of light, and the children of the day: we are not of the night, nor of darkness." 1 Thessalonians 5:2-5.

Thus it was shown that Scripture gives no warrant for men to remain in ignorance concerning the nearness of Christ's coming. But those who desired only an excuse to reject the truth closed their ears to this explanation, and the words "No man knoweth the day nor the hour" continued to be echoed by the bold scoffer and even by the professed minister of Christ. As the people were roused, and began to inquire the way of salvation, religious teachers stepped in between them and the truth, seeking to quiet their fears by falsely interpreting the word of God. Unfaithful watchmen united in the work of the great deceiver, crying, Peace, peace, when God had not spoken peace. Like the Pharisees in Christ's day, many refused to enter the kingdom of heaven themselves, and those who were entering in they hindered. The blood of these souls will be required at their hand.

The most humble and devoted in the churches were usually the first to receive the message. Those who studied the Bible for themselves could not but see the unscriptural character of the popular views of prophecy; and wherever the people were not controlled by the influence of the clergy, wherever they would search the word of God for themselves, the advent doctrine needed only to be compared with the Scriptures to establish its divine authority.

Many were persecuted by their unbelieving brethren. In order to retain their position in the church, some consented to be silent in regard to their hope; but others felt that loyalty to God forbade them thus to hide the truths which He had committed to their trust. Not a few were cut off from the fellowship of the church for no other reason than expressing their belief in the coming of Christ. Very precious to those who bore this trial of their faith were the words of the prophet: "Your brethren that hated you, that cast you out for My name's sake, said, Let the Lord be glorified: but He shall appear to your joy, and they shall be ashamed." Isaiah 66:5.

Angels of God were watching with the deepest interest the result of the warning. When there was a general rejection of the message by the churches, angels turned away in sadness. But there were many who had not yet been tested in regard to the advent truth. Many were misled by husbands, wives, parents, or children, and were made to believe it a sin even to listen to such heresies as were taught by the Adventists. Angels were bidden to keep faithful watch over these souls, for another light was yet to shine upon them from the throne of God.

With unspeakable desire those who had received the message watched for the coming of their Saviour. The time when they expected to meet Him was at hand. They approached this hour with a calm solemnity. They rested in sweet communion with God, and earnest of the peace that was to be theirs in the bright hereafter. None who experienced this hope and trust can forget those precious hours of waiting. For some weeks preceding the time, worldly business was for the most part laid aside. The sincere believers carefully examined every thought and emotion of their hearts as if upon their deathbeds and in a few hours to close their eyes upon earthly scenes. There was no making of "ascension robes"; but all felt the need of internal evidence that they were prepared to meet the Saviour; their white robes were purity of soul—characters cleansed from sin by the atoning blood of Christ. Would that there were still with the professed people of God the same spirit of heart searching, the same earnest, determined faith. Had they continued thus to humble themselves before the Lord and press their petitions at the mercy seat they would be in possession of a far richer experience than they now have. There is too little prayer, too little real conviction of sin, and the lack of living faith leaves many destitute of the grace so richly provided by our Redeemer.

God designed to prove His people. His hand covered a mistake in the reckoning of the prophetic periods. Adventists did not discover the error, nor was it discovered by the most learned of their opponents. The latter said: "Your reckoning of the prophetic periods is correct. Some great event is about to take place; but it is not what Mr. Miller predicts; it is the conversion of the world, and not the second advent of Christ."

The time of expectation passed, and Christ did not appear for the deliverance of His people. Those who with sincere faith and love had looked for their Saviour, experienced a bitter disappointment. Yet the purposes of God were being accomplished; He was testing the hearts of those who professed to be waiting for His appearing. There were among them many who had been actuated by no higher motive than fear. Their profession of faith had not affected their hearts or their lives. When the expected event failed to take place, these persons declared that they were not disappointed; they had never believed that Christ would come. They were among the first to ridicule the sorrow of the true believers.

But Jesus and all the heavenly host looked with love and sympathy upon the tried and faithful yet disappointed ones. Could the veil separating the visible from the invisible world have been swept back, angels would have been seen drawing near to these steadfast souls and shielding them from the shafts of Satan.

Six

—A Warning Rejected—

In preaching the doctrine of the second advent, William Miller and his associates had labored with the sole purpose of arousing men to a preparation for the judgment. They had sought to awaken professors of religion to the true hope of the church and to their need of a deeper Christian experience, and they labored also to awaken the unconverted to the duty of immediate repentance and conversion to God. "They made no attempt to convert men to a sect or party in religion. Hence they labored among all parties and sects, without interfering with their organization or discipline."

"In all my labors," said Miller, "I never had the desire or thought to establish any separate interest from that of existing denominations, or to benefit one at the expense of another. I thought to benefit all. Supposing that all Christians would rejoice in the prospect of Christ's coming, and that those who could not see as I did would not love any the less those who should embrace this doctrine, I did not conceive there would ever be any necessity for separate meetings. My whole object was a desire to convert souls to God, to notify the world of a coming judgment, and to induce my fellow men to make that preparation of heart which will enable them to meet their God in peace. The great majority of those who were converted under my labors united with the various existing churches."—Bliss, page 328.

As his work tended to build up the churches, it was for a time regarded with favor. But as ministers and religious leaders decided against the advent doctrine and desired to suppress all agitation of the subject, they not only opposed it from the pulpit, but denied their members the privilege of attending preaching upon the second advent, or even of speaking of their hope in the social meetings of the church. Thus the believers found themselves in a position of great trial and perplexity.

They loved their churches and were loath to separate from them; but as they saw the testimony of God's word suppressed and their right to investigate the prophecies denied they felt that loyalty to God forbade them to submit. Those who sought to shut out the testimony of God's word they could not regard as constituting the church of Christ, "the pillar and ground of the truth." Hence they felt themselves justified in separating from their former connection. In the summer of 1844 about fifty thousand withdrew from the churches.

About this time a marked change was apparent in most of the churches throughout the United States. There had been for many years a gradual but steadily increasing conformity to worldly practices and customs, and a corresponding decline in real spiritual life; but in that year there were evidences of a sudden and marked declension in nearly all the churches of the land. While none seemed able to suggest the cause, the fact itself was widely noted and commented upon by both the press and the pulpit.

At a meeting of the presbytery of Philadelphia, Mr. Barnes, author of a commentary widely used and pastor of one of the leading churches in that city, "stated that he had been in the ministry for twenty years, and never, till the last Communion, had he administered the ordinance without receiving more or less into the church. But now there are *no awakenings, no conversions*, not much apparent growth in grace in professors, and none come to his study to converse about the salvation of their souls. With the increase of business, and the brightening prospects of commerce and manufacture, there is an increase of worldly-mindedness. *Thus it is with all the denominations.*"—*Congregational Journal*, May 23, 1844.

In the month of February of the same year, Professor Finney of Oberlin College said: "We have had the fact before our minds, that, in general, the Protestant churches of our country, as such, were either apathetic or hostile to nearly all the moral reforms of the age. There are partial exceptions, yet not enough to render the fact otherwise than general. We have also another corroborated fact: the almost universal absence of revival influence in the churches. The spiritual apathy is almost all-pervading, and is fearfully deep; so the religious press of the whole land testifies. ... Very extensively, church members are becoming devotees of fashion,—join hands with the ungodly in parties of pleasure, in dancing, in festivities, etc. ... But we need not expand this painful subject. Suffice it that the evidence thickens and rolls heavily upon us, to show that the *churches generally are becoming sadly degenerate*. They have gone very far from the Lord, and He has withdrawn Himself from them."

And a writer in the *Religious Telescope* testified: "We have never witnessed such a general declension of religion as at the present. Truly, the church should awake, and search into the cause of this affliction; for as an affliction everyone that loves Zion must view it. When we call to mind how 'few and far between' cases of true conversion are, and the almost unparalleled impertinence and hardness of sinners, we almost involuntarily exclaim, 'Has God forgotten to be gracious? or, Is the door of mercy closed?'"

Such a condition never exists without cause in the church itself. The spiritual darkness which falls upon nations, upon churches and individuals, is due, not to an arbitrary withdrawal of the succors of divine grace on the part of God, but to neglect or rejection of divine light on the part of men. A striking illustration of this truth is presented in the history of the Jewish people in the time of Christ. By their devotion to the world and forgetfulness of God and His word, their understanding had become darkened, their hearts earthly and sensual. Thus they were in ignorance concerning Messiah's advent, and in their pride and unbelief they rejected the Redeemer. God did not even then cut off the Jewish nation from a knowledge of, or a participation in, the blessings of salvation. But those who rejected the truth lost all desire for the gift of Heaven. They had "put darkness for light, and light for darkness," until the light which was in them became darkness; and how great was that darkness!

It suits the policy of Satan that men should retain the forms of religion if but the spirit of vital godliness is lacking. After their rejection of the gospel, the Jews continued zealously to maintain their ancient rites, they rigorously preserved their national exclusiveness, while they themselves could not but admit that the presence of God was no longer manifest among them. The prophecy of Daniel pointed so unmistakably to the time of Messiah's coming, and so directly foretold His death, that they discouraged its study, and finally the rabbis pronounced a curse on all who should attempt a computation of the time. In blindness and impenitence the people of Israel during succeeding centuries have stood, indifferent to the gracious offers of salvation, unmindful of the blessings of the gospel, a solemn and fearful warning of the danger of rejecting light from heaven.

Wherever the cause exists, the same results will follow. He who deliberately stifles his convictions of duty because it interferes with his inclinations will finally lose the power to distinguish between truth and error. The understanding becomes darkened, the conscience callous, the heart hardened, and the soul is separated from God. Where the message of divine truth is spurned or slighted, there the church will be enshrouded in darkness; faith and love grow cold, and estrangement and dissension enter. Church members center their interests and energies in worldly pursuits, and sinners become hardened in their impenitence.

The first angel's message of Revelation 14, announcing the hour of God's judgment and calling upon men to fear and worship Him, was designed to separate the professed people of God from the corrupting influences of the world and to arouse them to see their true condition of worldliness and backsliding. In this message, God has sent to the church a warning, which, had it been accepted, would have corrected the evils that were shutting them away from Him. Had they received the message from heaven, humbling their hearts before the Lord and seeking in sincerity a preparation to stand in His presence, the Spirit and power of God would have been manifested among them. The church would again have reached that blessed state of unity, faith, and love which existed in apostolic days, when the believers "were of one heart and of one soul," and "spake the word of God with boldness," when "the Lord added to the church daily such as should be saved." Acts 4:32, 31; 2:47.

If God's professed people would receive the light as it shines upon them from His word, they would reach that unity for which Christ prayed, that which the apostle describes, "the unity of the Spirit in the bond of peace." "There is," he says, "*one* body, and *one* Spirit, even as ye are called in *one* hope of your calling; one Lord, one faith, one baptism." Ephesians 4:3-5.

Such were the blessed results experienced by those who accepted the advent message. They came from different denominations, and their denominational barriers were hurled to the ground; conflicting creeds were shivered to atoms; the unscriptural hope of a temporal millennium was abandoned, false views of the second advent were corrected, pride and conformity to the world were swept away; wrongs were made right; hearts were united in the sweetest fellowship, and love and joy reigned supreme. If this doctrine did this for the few who did receive it, it would have done the same for all if all had received it.

But the churches generally did not accept the warning. Their ministers, who, as watchmen "unto the house of Israel," should have been the first to discern the tokens of Jesus' coming, had failed to learn the truth either from the testimony of the prophets or from the signs of the times. As worldly hopes and ambitions filled the heart, love for God and faith in His word had grown cold; and when the advent doctrine was presented, it only aroused their prejudice and unbelief. The fact that the message was, to a great extent, preached by laymen, was urged as an argument against it. As of old, the plain testimony of God's word was met with the inquiry: "Have any of the rulers or of the Pharisees believed?" And finding how difficult a task it was to refute the arguments drawn from the prophetic periods, many discouraged the study of the prophecies, teaching that the prophetic books were sealed and were not to be understood. Multitudes, trusting implicitly to their pastors, refused to listen to the warning; and others, though convinced of the truth, dared not confess it, lest they should be "put out of the synagogue." The message which God had sent for the testing and purification of the church revealed all too surely how great was the number who had set their affections on this world rather than upon Christ. The ties which bound them to earth were stronger than the attractions heavenward. They chose to listen to the voice of worldly wisdom and turned away from the heart-searching message of truth.

In refusing the warning of the first angel, they rejected the means which Heaven had provided for their restoration. They spurned the gracious messenger that would have corrected the evils which separated them from God, and with greater eagerness they turned to seek the friendship of the world. Here was the cause of that fearful condition of worldliness, backsliding, and spiritual death which existed in the churches in 1844.

In Revelation 14 the first angel is followed by a second proclaiming: "Babylon is fallen, is fallen, that great city, because she made all nations drink of the wine of the wrath of her fornication." Revelation 14:8. The term "Babylon" is derived from "Babel," and signifies confusion. It is employed in Scripture to designate the various forms of false or apostate religion. In Revelation 17 Babylon is represented as a woman—a figure which is used in the Bible as the symbol of a church, a virtuous woman representing a pure church, a vile woman an apostate church.

In the Bible the sacred and enduring character of the relation that exists between Christ and His church is represented by the union of marriage. The Lord has joined His people to Himself by a solemn covenant, He promising to be their God, and they pledging themselves to be His and His alone. He declares: "I will betroth thee unto Me forever; yea, I will betroth thee unto Me in righteousness, and in judgment, and in loving-kindness, and in mercies." Hosea 2:19. And, again: "I am married unto you." Jeremiah 3:14. And Paul employs the same figure in the New Testament when he says: "I have espoused you to one husband, that I may present you as a chaste virgin to Christ." 2 Corinthians 11:2.

The unfaithfulness of the church to Christ in permitting her confidence and affection to be turned from Him, and allowing the love of worldly things to occupy the soul, is likened to the violation of the marriage vow. The sin of Israel in departing from the Lord is presented under this figure; and the wonderful love of God which they thus despised is touchingly portrayed: "I sware unto thee, and entered into a covenant with thee, saith the Lord God, and thou becamest Mine." "And thou wast exceeding beautiful and thou didst prosper into a kingdom. And thy renown went forth among the heathen for thy beauty: for it was perfect through My comeliness, which I had put upon thee. ... But thou didst trust in thine own beauty, and playedst the harlot because of thy renown." "As a wife treacherously departeth from her husband, so have ye dealt treacherously with Me, O house of Israel, saith the Lord;" "as a wife that committeth adultery, which taketh strangers instead of her husband!" Ezekiel 16:8, 13-15, 32; Jeremiah 3:20.

In the New Testament, language very similar is addressed to professed Christians who seek the friendship of the world above the favor of God. Says the apostle James: "Ye adulterers and adulteresses, know ye not that the friendship of the world is enmity with God? whosoever therefore will be a friend of the world is the enemy of God."

The woman (Babylon) of Revelation 17 is described as "arrayed in purple and scarlet color, and decked with gold and precious stones and pearls, having a golden cup in her hand full of abominations and filthiness: ... and upon her forehead was a name written, *Mystery, Babylon the Great, the mother of harlots.*" Says the prophet: "I saw the woman drunk with the blood of the saints, and with the blood of the martyrs of Jesus." Babylon is further declared to be "that great city, which reigneth over the kings of the earth." Revelation 17:4-6, 18. The power that for so many centuries maintained despotic sway over the monarchs of Christendom is Rome. The purple and scarlet color, the gold and precious stones and pearls, vividly picture the magnificence and more than kingly pomp affected by the haughty see of Rome. And no other power could be so truly declared "drunken with the blood of the saints" as that church which has so cruelly persecuted the followers of Christ. Babylon is also charged with the sin of unlawful connection with "the kings of the earth." It was by departure from the Lord, and alliance with the heathen, that the Jewish church became a harlot; and Rome, corrupting herself in like manner by seeking the support of worldly powers, receives a like condemnation.

Babylon is said to be "the *mother* of harlots." By her *daughters* must be symbolized churches that cling to her doctrines and traditions, and follow her example of sacrificing the truth and the approval of God, in order to form an unlawful alliance with the world. The message of Revelation 14, announcing the *fall* of Babylon must apply to religious bodies that were once pure and have become corrupt. Since this message follows the warning of the judgment, it must be given in the last days; therefore it cannot refer to the Roman Church alone, for that church has been in a fallen condition for many centuries. Furthermore, in the eighteenth chapter of the Revelation the people of God are called upon to come out of Babylon. According to this scripture, many of God's people must still be in Babylon. And in what religious bodies are the greater part of the followers of Christ now to be found? Without doubt, in the various churches professing the Protestant faith. At the time of their rise these churches took a noble stand for God and the truth, and His blessing was with them. Even the unbelieving world was constrained to acknowledge the beneficent results that followed an acceptance of the principles of the gospel. In the words of the prophet to Israel: "Thy renown went forth among the heathen for thy beauty: for it was perfect through My comeliness, which I had put upon thee, saith the Lord God." But they fell by the same desire which was the curse and ruin of Israel—the desire of imitating the practices and courting the friendship of the ungodly. "Thou didst trust in thine own beauty, and playedst the harlot because of thy renown." Ezekiel 16:14, 15.

Many of the Protestant churches are following Rome's example of iniquitous connection with "the kings of the earth"—the state churches, by their relation to secular governments; and other denominations, by seeking the favor of the world. And the term "Babylon"—confusion—may be appropriately applied to these bodies, all professing to derive their doctrines from the Bible, yet divided into almost innumerable sects, with widely conflicting creeds and theories.

Besides a sinful union with the world, the churches that separated from Rome present other of her characteristics.

A Roman Catholic work argues that "if the Church of Rome were ever guilty of idolatry in relation to the saints, her daughter, the Church of England, stands guilty of the same, which has ten churches dedicated to Mary for one dedicated to Christ."—Richard Challoner, *The Catholic Christian Instructed*, Preface, pages 21, 22.

And Dr. Hopkins, in "A Treatise on the Millennium," declares: "There is no reason to consider the antichristian spirit and practices to be confined to that which is now called the Church of Rome. The Protestant churches have much of antichrist in them, and are far from being wholly reformed from … corruptions and wickedness."—Samuel Hopkins, *Works*, vol. 2, p. 328.

Concerning the separation of the Presbyterian Church from Rome, Dr. Guthrie writes: "Three hundred years ago, our church, with an open Bible on her banner, and this motto, 'Search the Scriptures,' on her scroll, marched out from the gates of Rome." Then he asks the significant question: "Did they come *clean* out of Babylon?"—Thomas Guthrie, *The Gospel in Ezekiel*, page 237.

"The Church of England," says Spurgeon, "seems to be eaten through and through with sacramentarianism; but nonconformity appears to be almost as badly riddled with philosophical infidelity. Those of whom we thought better things are turning aside one by one from the fundamentals of the faith. Through and through, I believe, the very heart of England is honeycombed with a damnable infidelity which dares still go into the pulpit and call itself Christian."

What was the origin of the great apostasy? How did the church first depart from the simplicity of the gospel? By conforming to the practices of paganism, to facilitate the acceptance of Christianity by the heathen. The apostle Paul declared, even in his day, "The mystery of iniquity doth already work." 2 Thessalonians 2:7. During the lives of the apostles the church remained comparatively pure. But "toward the latter end of the second century most of the churches assumed a new form; the first simplicity disappeared, and insensibly, as the old disciples retired to their graves, their children, along with new converts, … came forward and new-modeled the cause."—Robert Robinson, *Ecclesiastical Researches*, ch. 6, par. 17, p. 51. To secure converts, the exalted standard of the Christian faith was lowered, and as the result "a pagan flood, flowing into the church, carried with it its customs, practices, and idols."—Gavazzi, *Lectures*, page 278. As the Christian religion secured the favor and support of secular rulers, it was nominally accepted by multitudes; but while in appearance Christians, many "remained in substance pagans, especially worshiping in secret their idols."—*Ibid.*, page 278.

Has not the same process been repeated in nearly every church calling itself Protestant? As the founders, those who possessed the true spirit of reform, pass away, their descendants come forward and "new-model the cause." While blindly clinging to the creed of their fathers and refusing to accept any truth in advance of what they saw, the children of the reformers depart widely from their example of humility, self-denial, and renunciation of the world. Thus "the first simplicity disappears." A worldly flood, flowing into the church, carries "with it its customs, practices, and idols."

Alas, to what a fearful extent is that friendship of the world which is "enmity with God," now cherished among the professed followers of Christ! How widely have the popular churches throughout Christendom departed from the Bible standard of humility, self-denial, simplicity, and godliness! Said John Wesley, in speaking of the right use of money: "Do not waste any part of so precious a talent, merely in gratifying the desire of the eye, by superfluous or expensive apparel, or by needless ornaments. Waste no part of it in curiously adorning your houses; in superfluous or expensive furniture; in costly pictures, painting, gilding. … Lay out nothing to gratify the pride of life, to gain the admiration or praise of men. … 'So long as thou doest well unto thyself, men will speak good of thee.' So long as thou art 'clothed in purple and fine linen,' and farest 'sumptuously every day,' no doubt many will applaud thy elegance of taste, thy generosity and hospitality. But do not buy their applause so dear. Rather be content with the honor that cometh from God."—Wesley, *Works*, Sermon 50, "The Use of Money." But in many churches of our time such teaching is disregarded.

A profession of religion has become popular with the world. Rulers, politicians, lawyers, doctors, merchants, join the church as a means of securing the respect and confidence of society, and advancing their own worldly interests. Thus they seek to cover all their unrighteous transactions under a profession of Christianity. The various religious bodies, re-enforced by the wealth and influence of these baptized worldlings, make a still higher bid for popularity and patronage. Splendid churches, embellished in the most extravagant manner, are erected on popular avenues. The worshipers array themselves in costly and fashionable attire. A high salary is paid for a talented minister to entertain and attract the people. His sermons must not touch popular sins, but be made smooth and pleasing for fashionable ears. Thus fashionable sinners are enrolled on the church records, and fashionable sins are concealed under a pretense of godliness.

Commenting on the present attitude of professed Christians toward the world, a leading secular journal says: "Insensibly the church has yielded to the spirit of the age, and adapted its forms of worship to modern wants." "All things, indeed, that help to make religion attractive, the church now employs as its instruments." And a writer in the New York *Independent* speaks thus concerning Methodism as it is: "The line of separation between the godly and the irreligious fades out into a kind of penumbra, and zealous men on both sides are toiling to obliterate all difference between their modes of action and enjoyment." "The popularity of religion tends vastly to increase the number of those who would secure its benefits without squarely meeting its duties."

Says Howard Crosby: "It is a matter of deep concern that we find Christ's church so little fulfilling the designs of its Lord. Just as the ancient Jews let a familiar intercourse with the idolatrous nations steal away their hearts from God, ... so the church of Jesus now is, by its false partnerships with an unbelieving world, giving up the divine methods of its true life, and yielding itself to the pernicious, though often plausible, habits of a Christless society, using the arguments and reaching the conclusions which are foreign to the revelation of God, and directly antagonistic to all growth in grace."—*The Healthy Christian: An Appeal to the Church*, pages 141, 142.

In this tide of worldliness and pleasure seeking, self-denial and self-sacrifice for Christ's sake are almost wholly lost. "Some of the men and women now in active life in our churches were educated, when children, to make sacrifices in order to be able to give or do something for Christ." But "if funds are wanted now, ... nobody must be called on to give. Oh, no! have a fair, tableau, mock trial, antiquarian supper, or something to eat—anything to amuse the people."

Governor Washburn of Wisconsin in his annual message, January 9, 1873, declared: "Some law seems to be required to break up the schools where gamblers are made. These are everywhere. Even the church (unwittingly, no doubt) is sometimes found doing the work of the devil. Gift concerts, gift enterprises and raffles, sometimes in aid of religious or charitable objects, but often for less worthy purposes, lotteries, prize packages, etc., are all devices to obtain money without value received. Nothing is so demoralizing or intoxicating, particularly to the young, as the acquisition of money or property without labor. Respectable people engaging in these chance enterprises, and easing their consciences with the reflection that the money is to go to a good object, it is not strange that the youth of the state should so often fall into the habits which the excitement of games of hazard is almost certain to engender."

The spirit of worldly conformity is invading the churches throughout Christendom. Robert Atkins, in a sermon preached in London, draws a dark picture of the spiritual declension that prevails in England: "The truly righteous are diminished from the earth, and no man layeth it to heart. The professors of religion of the present day, in every church, are lovers of the world, conformers to the world, lovers of creature comfort, and aspirers after respectability. They are called to suffer with Christ, but they shrink from even reproach. ... *Apostasy, apostasy, apostasy,* is engraven on the very front of every church; and did they know it, and did they feel it, there might be hope; but, alas! they cry, 'We are rich, and increased in goods, and stand in need of nothing.' "—Second Advent Library, tract No. 39.

The great sin charged against Babylon is that she "made all nations drink of the wine of the wrath of her fornication." This cup of intoxication which she presents to the world represents the false doctrines that she has accepted as the result of her unlawful connection with the great ones of the earth. Friendship with the world corrupts her faith, and in her turn she exerts a corrupting influence upon the world by teaching doctrines which are opposed to the plainest statements of Holy Writ.

Rome withheld the Bible from the people and required all men to accept her teachings in its place. It was the work of the Reformation to restore to men the word of God; but is it not too true that in the churches of our time men are taught to rest their faith upon their creed and the teachings of their church rather than on the Scriptures? Said Charles Beecher, speaking of the Protestant churches: "They shrink from any rude word against creeds with the same sensitiveness with which those holy fathers would have shrunk from a rude word against the rising veneration of saints and martyrs which they were fostering. ... The Protestant evangelical denominations have so tied up one another's hands, and their own, that, between them all, a man cannot become a preacher at all, anywhere, without accepting some book besides the Bible. ... There is nothing imaginary in the statement that the creed power is now beginning to prohibit the Bible as really as Rome did, though in a subtler way."—Sermon on "The Bible a Sufficient Creed," delivered at Fort Wayne, Indiana, Feb. 22, 1846.

When faithful teachers expound the word of God, there arise men of learning, ministers professing to understand the Scriptures, who denounce sound doctrine as heresy, and thus turn away inquirers after truth. Were it not that the world is hopelessly intoxicated with the wine of Babylon, multitudes would be convicted and converted by the plain, cutting truths of the word of God. But religious faith appears so confused and discordant that the people know not what to believe as truth. The sin of the world's impenitence lies at the door of the church.

The second angel's message of Revelation 14 was first preached in the summer of 1844, and it then had a more direct application to the churches of the United States, where the warning of the judgment had been most widely proclaimed and most generally rejected, and where the declension in the churches had been most rapid. But the message of the second angel did not reach its complete fulfillment in 1844. The churches then experienced a moral fall, in consequence of their refusal of the light of the advent message; but that fall was not complete. As they have continued to reject the special truths for this time they have fallen lower and lower. Not yet, however, can it be said that "Babylon is fallen, ... because she made *all nations* drink of the wine of the wrath of her fornication." She has not yet made all nations do this. The spirit of world conforming and indifference to the testing truths for our time exists and has been gaining ground in churches of the Protestant faith in all the countries of Christendom; and these churches are included in the solemn and terrible denunciation of the second angel. But the work of apostasy has not yet reached its culmination.

The Bible declares that before the coming of the Lord, Satan will work "with *all* power and signs and lying wonders, and with all deceivableness of unrighteousness;" and they that "received not the love of the truth, that they might be saved," will be left to receive "strong delusion, that they should believe a lie." 2 Thessalonians 2:9-11. Not until this condition shall be reached, and the union of the church with the world shall be fully accomplished throughout Christendom, will the fall of Babylon be complete. The change is a progressive one, and the perfect fulfillment of Revelation 14:8 is yet future.

Notwithstanding the spiritual darkness and alienation from God that exist in the churches which constitute Babylon, the great body of Christ's true followers are still to be found in their communion. There are many of these who have never seen the special truths for this time. Not a few are dissatisfied with their present condition and are longing for clearer light. They look in vain for the image of Christ in the churches with which they are connected. As these bodies depart further and further from the truth, and ally themselves more closely with the world, the difference between the two classes will widen, and it will finally result in separation. The time will come when those who love God supremely can no longer remain in connection with such as are "lovers of pleasures more than lovers of God; having a form of godliness, but denying the power thereof."

Revelation 18 points to the time when, as the result of rejecting the threefold warning of Revelation 14:6-12, the church will have fully reached the condition foretold by the second angel, and the people of God still in Babylon will be called upon to separate from her communion. This message is the last that will ever be given to the world; and it will accomplish its work. When those that "believed not the truth, but had pleasure in unrighteousness" (2 Thessalonians 2:12), shall be left to receive strong delusion and to believe a lie, then the light of truth will shine upon all whose hearts are open to receive it, and all the children of the Lord that remain in Babylon will heed the call: "Come out of her, My people" (Revelation 18:4).

Seven

—Prophecies Fulfilled—

When the time passed at which the Lord's coming was first expected,—in the spring of 1844,—those who had looked in faith for His appearing were for a season involved in doubt and uncertainty. While the world regarded them as having been utterly defeated and proved to have been cherishing a delusion, their source of consolation was still the word of God. Many continued to search the Scriptures, examining anew the evidences of their faith and carefully studying the prophecies to obtain further light. The Bible testimony in support of their position seemed clear and conclusive. Signs which could not be mistaken pointed to the coming of Christ as near. The special blessing of the Lord, both in the conversion of sinners and the revival of spiritual life among Christians, had testified that the message was of Heaven. And though the believers could not explain their disappointment, they felt assured that God had led them in their past experience.

Interwoven with prophecies which they had regarded as applying to the time of the second advent was instruction specially adapted to their state of uncertainty and suspense, and encouraging them to wait patiently in the faith that what was now dark to their understanding would in due time be made plain.

Among these prophecies was that of Habakkuk 2:1-4: "I will stand upon my watch, and set me upon the tower, and will watch to see what He will say unto me, and what I shall answer when I am reproved. And the Lord answered me, and said, Write the vision, and make it plain upon tables, that he may run that readeth it. For the vision is yet for an appointed time, but at the end it shall speak, and not lie: though it tarry, wait for it; because it will surely come, it will not tarry. Behold, his soul which is lifted up is not upright in him: but the just shall live by his faith."

As early as 1842 the direction given in this prophecy to "write the vision, and make it plain upon tables, that he may run that readeth it," had suggested to Charles Fitch the preparation of a prophetic chart to illustrate the visions of Daniel and the Revelation. The publication of this chart was regarded as a fulfillment of the command given by Habakkuk. No one, however, then noticed that an apparent delay in the accomplishment of the vision—a tarrying time—is presented in the same prophecy. After the disappointment, this scripture appeared very significant: "The vision is yet for an appointed time, but at the end it shall speak, and not lie: though it tarry, wait for it; because it will surely come, it will not tarry. ... The just shall live by his *faith*."

A portion of Ezekiel's prophecy also was a source of strength and comfort to believers: "The word of the Lord came unto me, saying, Son of man, what is that proverb that ye have in the land of Israel, saying, The days are prolonged, and every vision faileth? Tell them therefore, Thus saith the Lord God. ... The days are at hand, and the effect of every vision. ... I will speak, and the word that I shall speak shall come to pass; it shall be no more prolonged." "They of the house of Israel say, The vision that he seeth is for many days to come, and he prophesieth of the times that are far off. Therefore say unto them, Thus saith the Lord God; There shall none of My words be prolonged any more, but the word which I have spoken shall be done." Ezekiel 12:21-25, 27, 28.

The waiting ones rejoiced, believing that He who knows the end from the beginning had looked down through the ages and, foreseeing their disappointment, had given them words of courage and hope. Had it not been for such portions of Scripture, admonishing them to wait with patience and to hold fast their confidence in God's word, their faith would have failed in that trying hour.

The parable of the ten virgins of Matthew 25 also illustrates the experience of the Adventist people. In Matthew 24, in answer to the question of His disciples concerning the sign of His coming and of the end of the world, Christ had pointed out some of the most important events in the history of the world and of the church from His first to His second advent; namely, the destruction of Jerusalem, the great tribulation of the church under the pagan and papal persecutions, the darkening of the sun and moon, and the falling of the stars. After this He spoke of His coming in His kingdom, and related the parable describing the two classes of servants who look for His appearing. Chapter 25 opens with the words: "*Then* shall the kingdom of heaven be likened unto ten virgins." Here is brought to view the church living in the last days, the same that is pointed out in the close of chapter 24. In this parable their experience is illustrated by the incidents of an Eastern marriage.

"Then shall the kingdom of heaven be likened unto ten virgins, which took their lamps, and went forth to meet the bridegroom. And five of them were wise, and five were foolish. They that were foolish took their lamps, and took no oil with them: but the wise took oil in their vessels with their lamps. While the bridegroom tarried, they all slumbered and slept. And at midnight there was a cry made, Behold, the bridegroom cometh; go ye out to meet him."

The coming of Christ, as announced by the first angel's message, was understood to be represented by the coming of the bridegroom. The widespread reformation under the proclamation of His soon coming, answered to the going forth of the virgins. In this parable, as in that of Matthew 24, two classes are represented. All had taken their lamps, the Bible, and by its light had gone forth to meet the Bridegroom. But while "they that were foolish took their lamps, and took no oil with them," "the wise took oil in their vessels with their lamps. The latter class had received the grace of God, the regenerating, enlightening power of the Holy Spirit, which renders His word a lamp to the feet and a light to the path. In the fear of God they had studied the Scriptures to learn the truth, and had earnestly sought for purity of heart and life. These had a personal experience, a faith in God and in His word, which could not be overthrown by disappointment and delay. Others "took their lamps, and took no oil with them." They had moved from impulse. Their fears had been excited by the solemn message, but they had depended upon the faith of their brethren, satisfied with the flickering light of good emotions, without a thorough understanding of the truth or a genuine work of grace in the heart. These had gone forth to meet the Lord, full of hope in the prospect of immediate reward; but they were not prepared for delay and disappointment. When trials came, their faith failed, and their lights burned dim.

"While the bridegroom tarried, they all slumbered and slept." By the tarrying of the bridegroom is represented the passing of the time when the Lord was expected, the disappointment, and the seeming delay. In this time of uncertainty, the interest of the superficial and halfhearted soon began to waver, and their efforts to relax; but those whose faith was based on a personal knowledge of the Bible had a rock beneath their feet, which the waves of disappointment could not wash away. "They all slumbered and slept;" one class in unconcern and abandonment of their faith, the other class patiently waiting till clearer light should be given. Yet in the night of trial the latter seemed to lose, to some extent, their zeal and devotion. The halfhearted and superficial could no longer lean upon the faith of their brethren. Each must stand or fall for himself.

About this time, fanaticism began to appear. Some who had professed to be zealous believers in the message rejected the word of God as the one infallible guide and, claiming to be led by the Spirit, gave themselves up to the control of their own feelings, impressions, and imaginations. There were some who manifested a blind and bigoted zeal, denouncing all who would not sanction their course. Their fanatical ideas and exercises met with no sympathy from the great body of Adventists; yet they served to bring reproach upon the cause of truth.

Satan was seeking by this means to oppose and destroy the work of God. The people had been greatly stirred by the advent movement, thousands of sinners had been converted, and faithful men were giving themselves to the work of proclaiming the truth, even in the tarrying time. The prince of evil was losing his subjects; and in order to bring reproach upon the cause of God, he sought to deceive some who professed the faith and to drive them to extremes. Then his agents stood ready to seize upon every error, every failure, every unbecoming act, and hold it up before the people in the most exaggerated light, to render Adventists and their faith odious. Thus the greater the number whom he could crowd in to make a profession of faith in the second advent while his power controlled their hearts, the greater advantage would he gain by calling attention to them as representatives of the whole body of believers.

Satan is "the accuser of the brethren," and it is his spirit that inspires men to watch for the errors and defects of the Lord's people, and to hold them up to notice, while their good deeds are passed by without a mention. He is always active when God is at work for the salvation of souls. When the sons of God come to present themselves before the Lord, Satan comes also among them. In every revival he is ready to bring in those who are unsanctified in heart and unbalanced in mind. When these have accepted some points of truth, and gained a place with believers, he works through them to introduce theories that will deceive the unwary. No man is proved to be a true Christian because he is found in company with the children of God, even in the house of worship and around the table of the Lord. Satan is frequently there upon the most solemn occasions in the form of those whom he can use as his agents.

The prince of evil contests every inch of ground over which God's people advance in their journey toward the heavenly city. In all the history of the church no reformation has been carried forward without encountering serious obstacles. Thus it was in Paul's day. Wherever the apostle raised up a church, there were some who professed to receive the faith, but who brought in heresies, that, if received, would eventually crowd out the love of the truth. Luther also suffered great perplexity and distress from the course of fanatical persons who claimed that God had spoken directly through them, and who therefore set their own ideas and opinions above the testimony of the Scriptures. Many who were lacking in faith and experience, but who had considerable self-sufficiency, and who loved to hear and tell some new thing, were beguiled by the pretensions of the new teachers, and they joined the agents of Satan in their work of tearing down what God had moved Luther to build up. And the Wesleys, and others who blessed the world by their influence and their faith, encountered at every step the wiles of Satan in pushing overzealous, unbalanced, and unsanctified ones into fanaticism of every grade.

William Miller had no sympathy with those influences that led to fanaticism. He declared, with Luther, that every spirit should be tested by the word of God. "The devil," said Miller, "has great power over the minds of some at the present day. And how shall we know what manner of spirit they are of? The Bible answers: 'By their fruits ye shall know them.' ... There are many spirits gone out into the world; and we are commanded to try the spirits. The spirit that does not cause us to live soberly, righteously, and godly, in this present world, is not the Spirit of Christ. I am more and more convinced that Satan has much to do in these wild movements. ... Many among us who pretend to be wholly sanctified, are following the traditions of men, and apparently are as ignorant of truth as others who make no such pretensions."—Bliss, pages 236, 237. "The spirit of error will lead us from the truth; and the Spirit of God will lead us into truth. But, say you, a man may be in an error, and think he has the truth. What then? We answer, The Spirit and word agree. If a man judges himself by the word of God, and finds a perfect harmony through the whole word, then he must believe he has the truth; but if he finds the spirit by which he is led does not harmonize with the whole tenor of God's law or Book, then let him walk carefully, lest he be caught in the snare of the devil."—*The Advent Herald and Signs of the Times Reporter*, vol. 8, No. 23 (Jan. 15, 1845). "I have often obtained more evidence of inward piety from a kindling eye, a wet cheek, and a choked utterance, than from all the noise in Christendom."—Bliss, page 282.

In the days of the Reformation its enemies charged all the evils of fanaticism upon the very ones who were laboring most earnestly against it. A similar course was pursued by the opposers of the advent movement. And not content with misrepresenting and exaggerating the errors of extremists and fanatics, they circulated unfavorable reports that had not the slightest semblance of truth. These persons were actuated by prejudice and hatred. Their peace was disturbed by the proclamation of Christ at the door. They feared it might be true, yet hoped it was not, and this was the secret of their warfare against Adventists and their faith.

The fact that a few fanatics worked their way into the ranks of Adventists is no more reason to decide that the movement was not of God than was the presence of fanatics and deceivers in the church in Paul's or Luther's day a sufficient excuse for condemning their work. Let the people of God arouse out of sleep and begin in earnest the work of repentance and reformation; let them search the Scriptures to learn the truth as it is in Jesus; let them make an entire consecration to God, and evidence will not be wanting that Satan is still active and vigilant. With all possible deception he will manifest his power, calling to his aid all the fallen angels of his realm.

It was not the proclamation of the second advent that caused fanaticism and division. These appeared in the summer of 1844, when Adventists were in a state of doubt and perplexity concerning their real position. The preaching of the first angel's message and of the "midnight cry" tended directly to repress fanaticism and dissension. Those who participated in these solemn movements were in harmony; their hearts were filled with love for one another and for Jesus, whom they expected soon to see. The one faith, the one blessed hope, lifted them above the control of any human influence, and proved a shield against the assaults of Satan.

"While the bridegroom tarried, they all slumbered and slept. And at midnight there was a cry made, Behold, the bridegroom cometh;

go ye out to meet him. Then all those virgins arose, and trimmed their lamps." Matthew 25:5-7. In the summer of 1844, midway between the time when it had been first thought that the 2,300 days would end, and the autumn of the same year, to which it was afterward found that they extended, the message was proclaimed in the very words of Scripture: "Behold, the Bridegroom cometh!"

That which led to this movement was the discovery that the decree of Artaxerxes for the restoration of Jerusalem, which formed the starting point for the period of the 2,300 days, went into effect in the autumn of the year 457 B.C., and not at the beginning of the year, as had been formerly believed. Reckoning from the autumn of 457, the 2,300 years terminate in the autumn of 1844.

Arguments drawn from the Old Testament types also pointed to the autumn as the time when the event represented by the "cleansing of the sanctuary" must take place. This was made very clear as attention was given to the manner in which the types relating to the first advent of Christ had been fulfilled.

The slaying of the Passover lamb was a shadow of the death of Christ. Says Paul: "Christ our Passover is sacrificed for us." 1 Corinthians 5:7. The sheaf of first fruits, which at the time of the Passover was waved before the Lord, was typical of the resurrection of Christ. Paul says, in speaking of the resurrection of the Lord and of all His people: "Christ the first fruits; afterward they that are Christ's at His coming." 1 Corinthians 15:23. Like the wave sheaf, which was the first ripe grain gathered before the harvest, Christ is the first fruits of that immortal harvest of redeemed ones that at the future resurrection shall be gathered into the garner of God.

These types were fulfilled, not only as to the event, but as to the time. On the fourteenth day of the first Jewish month, the very day and month on which for fifteen long centuries the Passover lamb had been slain, Christ, having eaten the Passover with His disciples, instituted that feast which was to commemorate His own death as "the Lamb of God, which taketh away the sin of the world." That same night He was taken by wicked hands to be crucified and slain. And as the antitype of the wave sheaf our Lord was raised from the dead on the third day, "the first fruits of them that slept," a sample of all the resurrected just, whose "vile body" shall be changed, and "fashioned like unto His glorious body." Verse 20; Philippians 3:21.

In like manner the types which relate to the second advent must be fulfilled at the time pointed out in the symbolic service. Under the Mosaic system the cleansing of the sanctuary, or the great Day of Atonement, occurred on the tenth day of the seventh Jewish month (Leviticus 16:29-34), when the high priest, having made an atonement for all Israel, and thus removed their sins from the sanctuary, came forth and blessed the people. So it was believed that Christ, our great High Priest, would appear to purify the earth by the destruction of sin and sinners, and to bless His waiting people with immortality. The tenth day of the seventh month, the great Day of Atonement, the time of the cleansing of the sanctuary, which in the year 1844 fell upon the twenty-second of October, was regarded as the time of the Lord's coming. This was in harmony with the proofs already presented that the 2,300 days would terminate in the autumn, and the conclusion seemed irresistible.

In the parable of Matthew 25 the time of waiting and slumber is followed by the coming of the bridegroom. This was in accordance with the arguments just presented, both from prophecy and from the types. They carried strong conviction of their truthfulness; and the "midnight cry" was heralded by thousands of believers.

Like a tidal wave the movement swept over the land. From city to city, from village to village, and into remote country places it went, until the waiting people of God were fully aroused. Fanaticism disappeared before this proclamation like early frost before the rising sun. Believers saw their doubt and perplexity removed, and hope and courage animated their hearts. The work was free from those extremes which are ever manifested when there is human excitement without the controlling influence of the word and Spirit of God. It was similar in character to those seasons of humiliation and returning unto the Lord which among ancient Israel followed messages of reproof from His servants. It bore the characteristics that mark the work of God in every age. There was little ecstatic joy, but rather deep searching of heart, confession of sin, and forsaking of the world. A preparation to meet the Lord was the burden of agonizing spirits. There was persevering prayer and unreserved consecration to God.

Said Miller in describing that work: "There is no great expression of joy: that is, as it were, suppressed for a future occasion, when all heaven and earth will rejoice together with joy unspeakable and full of glory. There is no shouting: that, too, is reserved for the shout from heaven. The singers are silent: they are waiting to join the angelic hosts, the choir from heaven. ... There is no clashing of sentiments: all are of one heart and of one mind."—Bliss, pages 270, 271.

Another who participated in the movement testified: "It produced everywhere the most deep searching of heart and humiliation of soul before the God of high heaven. It caused a weaning of affections from the things of this world, a healing of controversies and animosities, a confession of wrongs, a breaking down before God, and penitent, brokenhearted supplications to Him for pardon and acceptance. It caused self-abasement and prostration of soul, such as we never before witnessed. As God by Joel commanded, when the great day of God should be at hand, it produced a rending of hearts and not of garments, and a turning unto the Lord with fasting, and weeping, and mourning. As God said by Zechariah, a spirit of grace and supplication was poured out upon His children; they looked to Him whom they had pierced, there was a great mourning in the land, ... and those who were looking for the Lord afflicted their souls before Him."—Bliss, in *Advent Shield and Review*, vol. I, p. 271 (January, 1845).

Of all the great religious movements since the days of the apostles, none have been more free from human imperfection and the wiles of Satan than was that of the autumn of 1844. Even now, after the lapse of many years, all who shared in that movement and who have stood firm upon the platform of truth still feel the holy influence of that blessed work and bear witness that it was of God.

At the call, "The Bridegroom cometh; go ye out to meet Him," the waiting ones "arose and trimmed their lamps;" they studied the word of God with an intensity of interest before unknown. Angels were sent from heaven to arouse those who had become discouraged and prepare them to receive the message. The work did not stand in the wisdom and learning of men, but in the power of God. It was not the most talented, but the most humble and devoted, who were the first to hear and obey the call. Farmers left their crops standing in the fields, mechanics laid down their tools, and with tears and rejoicing went out to give the warning. Those who had formerly led in the cause were among the last to join in this movement. The churches in general closed their doors against this message, and a large company of those who received it withdrew from their connection. In the providence of God this proclamation united with the second angel's message and gave power to that work.

The message, "Behold, the Bridegroom cometh!" was not so much a matter of argument, though the Scripture proof was clear and conclusive. There went with it an impelling power that moved the soul. There was no doubt, no questioning. Upon the occasion of Christ's triumphal entry into Jerusalem the people who were assembled from all parts of the land to keep the feast flocked to the Mount of Olives, and as they joined the throng that were escorting Jesus they caught the inspiration of the hour and helped to swell the shout: "Blessed is He that cometh in the name of the Lord!" Matthew 21:9. In like manner did unbelievers who flocked to the Adventist meetings—some from curiosity, some merely to ridicule—feel the convincing power attending the message: "Behold, the Bridegroom cometh!"

At that time there was faith that brought answers to prayer—faith that had respect to the recompense of reward. Like showers of rain upon the thirsty earth, the Spirit of grace descended upon the earnest seekers. Those who expected soon to stand face to face with their Redeemer felt a solemn joy that was unutterable. The softening, subduing power of the Holy Spirit melted the heart as His blessing was bestowed in rich measure upon the faithful, believing ones.

Carefully and solemnly those who received the message came up to the time when they hoped to meet their Lord. Every morning they felt that it was their first duty to secure the evidence of their acceptance with God. Their hearts were closely united, and they prayed much with and for one another. They often met together in secluded places to commune with God, and the voice of intercession ascended to heaven from the fields and groves. The assurance of the Saviour's approval was more necessary to them than their daily food; and if a cloud darkened their minds, they did not rest until it was swept away. As they felt the witness of pardoning grace, they longed to behold Him whom their souls loved.

But again they were destined to disappointment. The time of expectation passed, and their Saviour did not appear. With unwavering confidence they had looked forward to His coming, and now they felt as did Mary when, coming to the Saviour's tomb and finding it empty, she exclaimed with weeping: "They have taken away my Lord, and I know not where they have laid Him." John 20:13.

A feeling of awe, a fear that the message might be true, had for a time served as a restraint upon the unbelieving world. After the passing of the time this did not at once disappear; at first they dared not triumph over the disappointed ones; but as no tokens of God's wrath were seen, they recovered from their fears and resumed their reproach and ridicule. A large class who had professed to believe in the Lord's soon coming, renounced their faith. Some who had been very confident were so deeply wounded in their pride that they felt like fleeing from the world. Like Jonah, they complained of God, and chose death rather than life. Those who had based their faith upon the opinions of others, and not upon the word of God, were now as ready again to change their views. The scoffers won the weak and cowardly to their ranks, and all these united in declaring that there could be no more fears or expectations now. The time had passed, the Lord had not come, and the world might remain the same for thousands of years.

The earnest, sincere believers had given up all for Christ and had shared His presence as never before. They had, as they believed, given their last warning to the world; and, expecting soon to be received into the society of their divine Master and the heavenly angels, they had, to a great extent, withdrawn from the society of those who did not receive the message. With intense desire they had prayed: "Come, Lord Jesus, and come quickly." But He had not come. And now to take up again the heavy burden of life's cares and perplexities, and to endure the taunts and sneers of a scoffing world, was a terrible trial of faith and patience.

Yet this disappointment was not so great as was that experienced by the disciples at the time of Christ's first advent. When Jesus rode triumphantly into Jerusalem, His followers believed that He was about to ascend the throne of David and deliver Israel from her oppressors. With high hopes and joyful anticipations they vied with one another in showing honor to their King. Many spread their outer garments as a carpet in His path, or strewed before Him the leafy branches of the palm. In their enthusiastic joy they united in the glad acclaim: "Hosanna to the Son of David!" When the Pharisees, disturbed and angered by this outburst of rejoicing, wished Jesus to rebuke His disciples, He replied: "If these should hold their peace, the stones would immediately cry out." Luke 19:40. Prophecy must be fulfilled. The disciples were accomplishing the purpose of God; yet they were doomed to a bitter disappointment. But a few days had passed ere they witnessed the Saviour's agonizing death, and laid Him in the tomb. Their expectations had not been realized in a single particular, and their hopes died with Jesus. Not till their Lord had come forth triumphant from the grave could they perceive that all had been foretold by prophecy, and "that Christ must needs have suffered, and risen again from the dead." Acts 17:3.

Five hundred years before, the Lord had declared by the prophet Zechariah: "Rejoice greatly, O daughter of Zion; shout, O daughter of Jerusalem: behold, thy King cometh unto thee: He is just, and having salvation; lowly, and riding upon an ass, and upon a colt the foal of an ass." Zechariah 9:9. Had the disciples realized that Christ was going to judgment and to death, they could not have fulfilled this prophecy.

In like manner Miller and his associates fulfilled prophecy and gave a message which Inspiration had foretold should be given to the world, but which they could not have given had they fully understood the prophecies pointing out their disappointment, and presenting another message to be preached to all nations before the Lord should come. The first and second angel's messages were given at the right time and accomplished the work which God designed to accomplish by them.

The world had been looking on, expecting that if the time passed and Christ did not appear, the whole system of Adventism would be given up. But while many, under strong temptation, yielded their faith, there were some who stood firm. The fruits of the advent movement, the spirit of humility and heart searching, of renouncing of the world and reformation of life, which had attended the work, testified that it was of God. They dared not deny that the power of the Holy Spirit had witnessed to the preaching of the second advent, and they could detect no error in their reckoning of the prophetic periods. The ablest of their opponents had not succeeded in overthrowing their system of prophetic interpretation. They could not consent, without Bible evidence, to renounce positions which had been reached through earnest, prayerful study of the Scriptures, by minds enlightened by the Spirit of God and hearts burning with its living power; positions which had withstood the most searching criticisms and the most bitter opposition of popular religious teachers and worldly-wise men, and which had stood firm against the combined forces of learning and eloquence, and the taunts and revilings alike of the honorable and the base.

True, there had been a failure as to the expected event, but even this could not shake their faith in the word of God. When Jonah proclaimed in the streets of Nineveh that within forty days the city would be overthrown, the Lord accepted the humiliation of the

Ninevites and extended their period of probation; yet the message of Jonah was sent of God, and Nineveh was tested according to His will. Adventists believed that in like manner God had led them to give the warning of the judgment. "It has," they declared, "tested the hearts of all who heard it, and awakened a love for the Lord's appearing; or it has called forth a hatred, more or less perceivable, but known to God, of His coming. It has drawn a line, ... so that those who will examine their own hearts, may know on which side of it they would have been found, had the Lord then come—whether they would have exclaimed, 'Lo! this is our God, we have waited for Him, and He will save us;' or whether they would have called to the rocks and mountains to fall on them to hide them from the face of Him that sitteth on the throne, and from the wrath of the Lamb. God thus, as we believe, has tested His people, has tried their faith, has proved them, and seen whether they would shrink, in the hour of trial, from the position in which He might see fit to place them; and whether they would relinquish this world and rely with implicit confidence in the word of God."—*The Advent Herald and Signs of the Times Reporter*, vol. 8, No. 14 (Nov 13, 1844).

The feelings of those who still believed that God had led them in their past experience are expressed in the words of William Miller: "Were I to live my life over again, with the same evidence that I then had, to be honest with God and man I should have to do as I have done." "I hope that I have cleansed my garments from the blood of souls. I feel that, as far as it was in my power, I have freed myself from all guilt in their condemnation." "Although I have been twice disappointed," wrote this man of God, "I am not yet cast down or discouraged. ... My hope in the coming of Christ is as strong as ever. I have done only what, after years of solemn consideration, I felt it my solemn duty to do. If I have erred, it has been on the side of charity, love to my fellow men, and conviction of duty to God." "One thing I do know, I have preached nothing but what I believed; and God has been with me; His power has been manifested in the work, and much good has been effected." "Many thousands, to all human appearance, have been made to study the Scriptures by the preaching of the time; and by that means, through faith and the sprinkling of the blood of Christ, have been reconciled to God."—Bliss, pages 256, 255, 277, 280, 281. "I have never courted the smiles of the proud, nor quailed when the world frowned. I shall not now purchase their favor, nor shall I go beyond duty to tempt their hate. I shall never seek my life at their hands, nor shrink, I hope, from losing it, if God in His good providence so orders."—J. White, *Life of Wm. Miller*, page 315.

God did not forsake His people; His Spirit still abode with those who did not rashly deny the light which they had received, and denounce the advent movement. In the Epistle to the Hebrews are words of encouragement and warning for the tried, waiting ones at this crisis: "Cast not away therefore your confidence, which hath great recompense of reward. For ye have need of patience, that, after ye have done the will of God, ye might receive the promise. For yet a little while, and He that shall come will come, and will not tarry. Now the just shall live by faith: but if any man draw back, My soul shall have no pleasure in him. But we are not of them who draw back unto perdition; but of them that believe to the saving of the soul." Hebrews 10:35-39.

That this admonition is addressed to the church in the last days is evident from the words pointing to the nearness of the Lord's coming: "For yet a little while, and He that shall come will come and will not tarry." And it is plainly implied that there would be a seeming delay and that the Lord would appear to tarry. The instruction here given is especially adapted to the experience of Adventists at this time. The people here addressed were in danger of making shipwreck of faith. They had done the will of God in following the guidance of His Spirit and His word; yet they could not understand His purpose in their past experience, nor could they discern the pathway before them, and they were tempted to doubt whether God had indeed been leading them. At this time the words were applicable: "Now the just shall live by faith." As the bright light of the "midnight cry" had shone upon their pathway, and they had seen the prophecies unsealed and the rapidly fulfilling signs telling that the coming of Christ was near, they had walked, as it were, by sight. But now, bowed down by disappointed hopes, they could stand only by faith in God and in His word. The scoffing world were saying: "You have been deceived. Give up your faith, and say that the advent movement was of Satan." But God's word declared: "If any man draw back, My soul shall have no pleasure in him." To renounce their faith now, and deny the power of the Holy Spirit which had attended the message, would be drawing back toward perdition. They were encouraged to steadfastness by the words of Paul: "Cast not away therefore your confidence;" "ye have need of patience," "for yet a little while, and He that shall come will come, and will not tarry." Their only safe course was to cherish the light which they had already received of God, hold fast to His promises, and continue to search the Scriptures, and patiently wait and watch to receive further light.

Eight

—What Is the Sanctuary?—

The scripture which above all others had been both the foundation and the central pillar of the advent faith was the declaration: "Unto two thousand and three hundred days; then shall the sanctuary be cleansed." Daniel 8:14. These had been familiar words to all believers in the Lord's soon coming. By the lips of thousands was this prophecy repeated as the watchword of their faith. All felt that upon the events therein foretold depended their brightest expectations and most cherished hopes. These prophetic days had been shown to terminate in the autumn of 1844. In common with the rest of the Christian world, Adventists then held that the earth, or some portion of it, was the sanctuary. They understood that the cleansing of the sanctuary was the purification of the earth by the fires of the last great day, and that this would take place at the second advent. Hence the conclusion that Christ would return to the earth in 1844.

But the appointed time had passed, and the Lord had not appeared. The believers knew that God's word could not fail; their interpretation of the prophecy must be at fault; but where was the mistake? Many rashly cut the knot of difficulty by denying that the 2,300 days ended in 1844. No reason could be given for this except that Christ had not come at the time they expected Him. They argued that if the prophetic days had ended in 1844, Christ would then have returned to cleanse the sanctuary by the purification of the earth by fire; and that since He had not come, the days could not have ended.

To accept this conclusion was to renounce the former reckoning of the prophetic periods. The 2,300 days had been found to begin when the commandment of Artaxerxes for the restoration and building of Jerusalem went into effect, in the autumn of 457 B.C. Taking this as the starting point, there was perfect harmony in the application of all the events foretold in the explanation of that period in Daniel 9:25-27. Sixty-nine weeks, the first 483 of the 2,300 years, were to reach to the Messiah, the Anointed One; and Christ's baptism and anointing by the Holy Spirit, A.D. 27, exactly fulfilled the specification. In the midst of the seventieth week, Messiah was to be cut off. Three and a half years after His baptism, Christ was crucified, in the spring of A.D. 31. The seventy weeks, or 490 years, were to pertain especially to the Jews. At the expiration of this period the nation sealed its rejection of Christ by the persecution of His disciples, and the apostles turned to the Gentiles, A.D. 34. The first 490 years of the 2,300 having then ended, 1,810 years would remain. From A.D. 34, 1,810 years extend to 1844. "Then," said the angel, "shall the sanctuary be cleansed." All the preceding specifications of the prophecy had been unquestionably fulfilled at the time appointed.

With this reckoning, all was clear and harmonious, except that it was not seen that any event answering to the cleansing of the sanctuary had taken place in 1844. To deny that the days ended at that time was to involve the whole question in confusion, and to renounce positions which had been established by unmistakable fulfillments of prophecy.

But God had led His people in the great advent movement; His power and glory had attended the work, and He would not permit it to end in darkness and disappointment, to be reproached as a false and fanatical excitement. He would not leave His word involved in doubt and uncertainty. Though many abandoned their former reckoning of the prophetic periods and denied the correctness of the movement based thereon, others were unwilling to renounce points of faith and experience that were sustained by the Scriptures and by the witness of the Spirit of God. They believed that they had adopted sound principles of interpretation in their study of the prophecies, and that it was their duty to hold fast the truths already gained, and to continue the same course of Biblical research. With earnest prayer they reviewed their position and studied the Scriptures to discover their mistake. As they could see no error in their reckoning of the prophetic periods, they were led to examine more closely the subject of the sanctuary.

In their investigation they learned that there is no Scripture evidence sustaining the popular view that the earth is the sanctuary; but they found in the Bible a full explanation of the subject of the sanctuary, its nature, location, and services; the testimony of the sacred writers being so clear and ample as to place the matter beyond all question. The apostle Paul, in the Epistle to the Hebrews, says: "Then verily the first covenant had also ordinances of divine service, and a worldly sanctuary. For there was a tabernacle made; the first, wherein was the candlestick, and the table, and the shewbread; which is called the sanctuary. And after the second veil, the tabernacle which is called the holiest of all; which had the golden censer, and the ark of the covenant overlaid round about with gold, wherein was the golden pot that had manna, and Aaron's rod that budded, and the tables of the covenant; and over it the cherubims of glory shadowing the mercy seat." Hebrews 9:1-5.

The sanctuary to which Paul here refers was the tabernacle built by Moses at the command of God as the earthly dwelling place of the Most High. "Let them make Me a sanctuary; that I may dwell among them" (Exodus 25:8), was the direction given to Moses while in the mount with God. The Israelites were journeying through the wilderness, and the tabernacle was so constructed that it could be removed from place to place; yet it was a structure of great magnificence. Its walls consisted of upright boards heavily plated with gold and set in sockets of silver, while the roof was formed of a series of curtains, or coverings, the outer of skins, the innermost of fine linen beautifully wrought with figures of cherubim. Besides the outer court, which contained the altar of burnt offering, the tabernacle itself consisted of two apartments called the holy and the most holy place, separated by a rich and beautiful curtain, or veil; a similar veil closed the entrance to the first apartment.

In the holy place was the candlestick, on the south, with its seven lamps giving light to the sanctuary both by day and by night; on the north stood the table of shewbread; and before the veil separating the holy from the most holy was the golden altar of incense, from which the cloud of fragrance, with the prayers of Israel, was daily ascending before God.

In the most holy place stood the ark, a chest of precious wood overlaid with gold, the depository of the two tables of stone upon which God had inscribed the law of Ten Commandments. Above the ark, and forming the cover to the sacred chest, was the mercy seat, a magnificent piece of workmanship, surmounted by two cherubim, one at each end, and all wrought of solid gold. In this apartment the divine presence was manifested in the cloud of glory between the cherubim.

After the settlement of the Hebrews in Canaan, the tabernacle was replaced by the temple of Solomon, which, though a permanent structure and upon a larger scale, observed the same proportions, and was similarly furnished. In this form the sanctuary existed—except while it lay in ruins in Daniel's time—until its destruction by the Romans, in A.D. 70.

This is the only sanctuary that ever existed on the earth, of which the Bible gives any information. This was declared by Paul to be the sanctuary of the first covenant. But has the new covenant no sanctuary?

Turning again to the book of Hebrews, the seekers for truth found that the existence of a second, or new-covenant sanctuary, was implied in the words of Paul already quoted: "Then verily the first covenant had *also* ordinances of divine service, and a worldly sanctuary." And the use of the word "also" intimates that Paul has before made mention of this sanctuary. Turning back to the beginning of the previous chapter, they read: "Now of the things which we have spoken this is the sum: We have such an High Priest, who is set on the right hand of the throne of the Majesty in the heavens; a Minister of the sanctuary, and of the true tabernacle, which the Lord pitched, and not man." Hebrews 8:1, 2.

Here is revealed the sanctuary of the new covenant. The sanctuary of the first covenant was pitched by man, built by Moses; this is pitched by the Lord, not by man. In that sanctuary the earthly priests performed their service; in this, Christ, our great High Priest, ministers at God's right hand. One sanctuary was on earth, the other is in heaven.

Further, the tabernacle built by Moses was made after a pattern. The Lord directed him: "According to all that I show thee, after the pattern of the tabernacle, and the pattern of all the instruments thereof, even so shall ye make it." And again the charge was given, "Look that thou make them after their pattern, which was showed thee in the mount." Exodus 25:9, 40. And Paul says that the first tabernacle "was a figure for the time then present, in which were offered both gifts and sacrifices;" that its holy places were "patterns of things in the heavens;" that the priests who offered gifts according to the law served "unto the example and shadow of heavenly things," and that "Christ is not entered into the holy places made with hands, which are the figures of the true; but into heaven itself, now to appear in the presence of God for us." Hebrews 9:9, 23; 8:5; 9:24.

The sanctuary in heaven, in which Jesus ministers in our behalf, is the great original, of which the sanctuary built by Moses was a copy. God placed His Spirit upon the builders of the earthly sanctuary. The artistic skill displayed in its construction was a manifestation of divine wisdom. The walls had the appearance of massive gold, reflecting in every direction the light of the seven lamps of the golden candlestick. The table of shewbread and the altar of incense glittered like burnished gold. The gorgeous curtain which formed the ceiling, inwrought with figures of angels in blue and purple and scarlet, added to the beauty of the scene. And beyond the second veil was the holy Shekinah, the visible manifestation of God's glory, before which none but the high priest could enter and live.

The matchless splendor of the earthly tabernacle reflected to human vision the glories of that heavenly temple where Christ our forerunner ministers for us before the throne of God. The abiding place of the King of kings, where thousand thousands minister unto Him, and ten thousand times ten thousand stand before Him (Daniel 7:10); that temple, filled with the glory of the eternal throne, where seraphim, its shining guardians, veil their faces in adoration, could find, in the most magnificent structure ever reared by human hands, but a faint reflection of its vastness and glory. Yet important truths concerning the heavenly sanctuary and the great work there carried forward for man's redemption were taught by the earthly sanctuary and its services.

The holy places of the sanctuary in heaven are represented by the two apartments in the sanctuary on earth. As in vision the apostle John was granted a view of the temple of God in heaven, he beheld there "seven lamps of fire burning before the throne." Revelation 4:5. He saw an angel "having a golden censer; and there was given unto him much incense, that he should offer it with the prayers of all saints upon the golden altar which was before the throne." Revelation 8:3. Here the prophet was permitted to behold the first apartment of the sanctuary in heaven; and he saw there the "seven lamps of fire" and "the golden altar," represented by the golden candlestick and the altar of incense in the sanctuary on earth. Again, "the temple of God was opened" (Revelation 11:19), and he looked within the inner veil, upon the holy of holies. Here he beheld "the ark of His testament," represented by the sacred chest constructed by Moses to contain the law of God.

Thus those who were studying the subject found indisputable proof of the existence of a sanctuary in heaven. Moses made the earthly sanctuary after a pattern which was shown him. Paul teaches that that pattern was the true sanctuary which is in heaven. And John testifies that he saw it in heaven.

In the temple in heaven, the dwelling place of God, His throne is established in righteousness and judgment. In the most holy place is His law, the great rule of right by which all mankind are tested. The ark that enshrines the tables of the law is covered with the mercy seat, before which Christ pleads His blood in the sinner's behalf. Thus is represented the union of justice and mercy in the plan of human redemption. This union infinite wisdom alone could devise and infinite power accomplish; it is a union that fills all heaven with wonder and adoration. The cherubim of the earthly sanctuary, looking reverently down upon the mercy seat, represent the interest with which the heavenly host contemplate the work of redemption. This is the mystery of mercy into which angels desire to look—that God can be just while He justifies the repenting sinner and renews His intercourse with the fallen race; that Christ could stoop to raise unnumbered multitudes from the abyss of ruin and clothe them with the spotless garments of His own righteousness to unite with angels who have never fallen and to dwell forever in the presence of God.

The work of Christ as man's intercessor is presented in that beautiful prophecy of Zechariah concerning Him "whose name is the Branch." Says the prophet: "He shall build the temple of the Lord; and He shall bear the glory, and shall sit and rule upon His [the Father's] throne; and He shall be a priest upon His throne: and the *counsel of peace* shall be between Them both." Zechariah 6:12, 13.

"He shall build the temple of the Lord." By His sacrifice and mediation Christ is both the foundation and the builder of the church of God. The apostle Paul points to Him as "the chief Cornerstone; in whom all the building fitly framed together groweth into an holy temple in the Lord: in whom ye also," he says, "are builded together for an habitation of God through the Spirit." Ephesians 2:20-22.

"He shall bear the glory." To Christ belongs the glory of redemption for the fallen race. Through the eternal ages, the song of the ransomed ones will be: "Unto Him that loved us, and washed us from our sins in His own blood, ... to Him be glory and dominion for ever and ever." Revelation 1:5, 6.

He "shall sit and rule upon His throne; and He shall be a priest upon His throne." Not now "upon the throne of His glory;" the kingdom of glory has not yet been ushered in. Not until His work as a mediator shall be ended will God "give unto Him the throne of His father David," a kingdom of which "there shall be no end." Luke 1:32,

33. As a priest, Christ is now set down with the Father in His throne. Revelation 3:21. Upon the throne with the eternal, self-existent One is He who "hath borne our griefs, and carried our sorrows," who "was in all points tempted like as we are, yet without sin," that He might be "able to succor them that are tempted." "If any man sin, we have an advocate with the Father." Isaiah 53:4; Hebrews 4:15; 2:18; 1 John 2:1. His intercession is that of a pierced and broken body, of a spotless life. The wounded hands, the pierced side, the marred feet, plead for fallen man, whose redemption was purchased at such infinite cost.

"And the counsel of peace shall be between Them both." The love of the Father, no less than of the Son, is the fountain of salvation for the lost race. Said Jesus to His disciples before He went away: "I say not unto you, that I will pray the Father for you: for the Father Himself loveth you." John 16:26, 27. God was "in Christ, reconciling the world unto Himself." 2 Corinthians 5:19. And in the ministration in the sanctuary above, "the counsel of peace shall be between Them both." "God *so loved* the world, that He gave His only-begotten Son, that whosoever believeth in Him should not perish, but have everlasting life." John 3:16.

The question, What is the sanctuary? is clearly answered in the Scriptures. The term "sanctuary," as used in the Bible, refers, first, to the tabernacle built by Moses, as a pattern of heavenly things; and, secondly, to the "true tabernacle" in heaven, to which the earthly sanctuary pointed. At the death of Christ the typical service ended. The "true tabernacle" in heaven is the sanctuary of the new covenant. And as the prophecy of Daniel 8:14 is fulfilled in this dispensation, the sanctuary to which it refers must be the sanctuary of the new covenant. At the termination of the 2,300 days, in 1844, there had been no sanctuary on earth for many centuries. Thus the prophecy, "Unto two thousand and three hundred days; then shall the sanctuary be cleansed," unquestionably points to the sanctuary in heaven.

But the most important question remains to be answered: What is the cleansing of the sanctuary? That there was such a service in connection with the earthly sanctuary is stated in the Old Testament Scriptures. But can there be anything in heaven to be cleansed? In Hebrews 9 the cleansing of both the earthly and the heavenly sanctuary is plainly taught. "Almost all things are by the law purged with blood; and without shedding of blood is no remission. It was therefore necessary that the patterns of things in the heavens should be purified with these [the blood of animals]; but the heavenly things themselves with better sacrifices than these" (Hebrews 9:22, 23), even the precious blood of Christ.

The cleansing, both in the typical and in the real service, must be accomplished with blood: in the former, with the blood of animals; in the latter, with the blood of Christ. Paul states, as the reason why this cleansing must be performed with blood, that without shedding of blood is no *remission*. Remission, or putting away of sin, is the work to be accomplished. But how could there be sin connected with the sanctuary, either in heaven or upon the earth? This may be learned by reference to the symbolic service; for the priests who officiated on earth, served "unto the example and shadow of heavenly things." Hebrews 8:5.

The ministration of the earthly sanctuary consisted of two divisions; the priests ministered daily in the holy place, while once a year the high priest performed a special work of atonement in the most holy, for the cleansing of the sanctuary. Day by day the repentant sinner brought his offering to the door of the tabernacle and, placing his hand upon the victim's head, confessed his sins, thus in figure transferring them from himself to the innocent sacrifice. The animal was then slain. "Without shedding of blood," says the apostle, there is no remission of sin. "The life of the flesh is in the blood." Leviticus 17:11. The broken law of God demanded the life of the transgressor. The blood, representing the forfeited life of the sinner, whose guilt the victim bore, was carried by the priest into the holy place and sprinkled before the veil, behind which was the ark containing the law that the sinner had transgressed. By this ceremony the sin was, through the blood, transferred in figure to the sanctuary. In some cases the blood was not taken into the holy place; but the flesh was then to be eaten by the priest, as Moses directed the sons of Aaron, saying: "God hath given it you to bear the iniquity of the congregation." Leviticus 10:17. Both ceremonies alike symbolized the transfer of the sin from the penitent to the sanctuary.

Such was the work that went on, day by day, throughout the year. The sins of Israel were thus transferred to the sanctuary, and a special work became necessary for their removal. God commanded that an atonement be made for each of the sacred apartments. "He shall make an atonement for the holy place, because of the uncleanness of the children of Israel, and because of their transgressions in all their sins: and so shall he do for the tabernacle of the congregation, that remaineth among them in the midst of their uncleanness." An atonement was also to be made for the altar, to "cleanse it, and hallow if from the uncleanness of the children of Israel." Leviticus 16:16, 19.

Once a year, on the great Day of Atonement, the priest entered the most holy place for the cleansing of the sanctuary. The work there performed completed the yearly round of ministration. On the Day of Atonement two kids of the goats were brought to the door of the tabernacle, and lots were cast upon them, "one lot for the Lord, and the other lot for the scapegoat." Verse 8. The goat upon which fell the lot for the Lord was to be slain as a sin offering for the people. And the priest was to bring his blood within the veil and sprinkle it upon the mercy seat and before the mercy seat. The blood was also to be sprinkled upon the altar of incense that was before the veil.

"And Aaron shall lay both his hands upon the head of the live goat, and confess over him all the iniquities of the children of Israel, and all their transgressions in all their sins, putting them upon the head of the goat, and shall send him away by the hand of a fit man into the wilderness: and the goat shall bear upon him all their iniquities unto a land not inhabited." Verses 21, 22. The scapegoat came no more into the camp of Israel, and the man who led him away was required to wash himself and his clothing with water before returning to the camp.

The whole ceremony was designed to impress the Israelites with the holiness of God and His abhorrence of sin; and, further, to show them that they could not come in contact with sin without becoming polluted. Every man was required to afflict his soul while this work of atonement was going forward. All business was to be laid aside, and the whole congregation of Israel were to spend the day in solemn humiliation before God, with prayer, fasting, and deep searching of heart.

Important truths concerning the atonement are taught by the typical service. A substitute was accepted in the sinner's stead; but the sin was not canceled by the blood of the victim. A means was thus provided by which it was transferred to the sanctuary. By the offering of blood the sinner acknowledged the authority of the law, confessed his guilt in transgression, and expressed his desire for pardon through faith in a Redeemer to come; but he was not yet entirely released from the condemnation of the law. On the Day of Atonement the high priest, having taken an offering from the congregation, went into the most holy place with the blood of this offering, and sprinkled it upon the mercy seat, directly over the law, to make satisfaction for its claims. Then, in his character of mediator, he took the sins upon himself and bore them from the sanctuary. Placing his hands upon the head of the scapegoat, he confessed over him all these sins, thus in figure transferring them from himself to the goat. The goat then bore them away, and they were regarded as forever separated from the people.

Such was the service performed "unto the example and shadow of heavenly things." And what was done in type in the ministration of the earthly sanctuary is done in reality in the ministration of the heavenly sanctuary. After His ascension our Saviour began His work as our high priest. Says Paul: "Christ is not entered into the holy places made with hands, which are the figures of the true; but into heaven itself, now to appear in the presence of God for us." Hebrews 9:24.

The ministration of the priest throughout the year in the first apartment of the sanctuary, "within the veil" which formed the door and separated the holy place from the outer court, represents the work of ministration upon which Christ entered at His ascension. It was the work of the priest in the daily ministration to present before God the blood of the sin offering, also the incense which ascended with the prayers of Israel. So did Christ plead His blood before the Father in behalf of sinners, and present before Him also, with the precious fragrance of His own righteousness, the prayers of penitent believers. Such was the work of ministration in the first apartment of the sanctuary in heaven.

Thither the faith of Christ's disciples followed Him as He ascended from their sight. Here their hopes centered, "which hope we have," said Paul, "as an anchor of the soul, both sure and steadfast, and which entereth into that within the veil; whither the forerunner is for us entered, even Jesus, made an high priest forever." "Neither by the blood of goats and calves, but by His own blood He entered in once into the holy place, having obtained eternal redemption for us." Hebrews 6:19, 20; 9:12.

For eighteen centuries this work of ministration continued in the first apartment of the sanctuary. The blood of Christ, pleaded in behalf of penitent believers, secured their pardon and acceptance with the Father, yet their sins still remained upon the books of record. As in the typical service there was a work of atonement at the close of the year, so before Christ's work for the redemption of men is completed there is a work of atonement for the removal of sin from the sanctuary. This is the service which began when the 2,300 days ended. At that time, as foretold by Daniel the prophet, our High Priest entered the most holy, to perform the last division of His solemn work—to cleanse the sanctuary.

As anciently the sins of the people were by faith placed upon the sin offering and through its blood transferred, in figure, to the earthly sanctuary, so in the new covenant the sins of the repentant are by faith placed upon Christ and transferred, in fact, to the heavenly sanctuary. And as the typical cleansing of the earthly was accomplished by the removal of the sins by which it had been polluted, so the actual cleansing of the heavenly is to be accomplished by the removal, or blotting out, of the sins which are there recorded. But before this can be accomplished, there must be an examination of the books of record to determine who, through repentance of sin and faith in Christ, are entitled to the benefits of His atonement. The cleansing of the sanctuary therefore involves a work of investigation—a work of judgment. This work must be performed prior to the coming of Christ to redeem His people; for when He comes, His reward is with Him to give to every man according to his works. Revelation 22:12.

Thus those who followed in the light of the prophetic word saw that, instead of coming to the earth at the termination of the 2,300 days in 1844, Christ then entered the most holy place of the heavenly sanctuary to perform the closing work of atonement preparatory to His coming.

It was seen, also, that while the sin offering pointed to Christ as a sacrifice, and the high priest represented Christ as a mediator, the scapegoat typified Satan, the author of sin, upon whom the sins of the truly penitent will finally be placed. When the high priest, by virtue of the blood of the sin offering, removed the sins from the sanctuary, he placed them upon the scapegoat. When Christ, by virtue of His own blood, removes the sins of His people from the heavenly sanctuary at the close of His ministration, He will place them upon Satan, who, in the execution of the judgment, must bear the final penalty. The scapegoat was sent away into a land not inhabited, never to come again into the congregation of Israel. So will Satan be forever banished from the presence of God and His people, and he will be blotted from existence in the final destruction of sin and sinners.

Nine

—In the Holy of Holies—

The subject of the sanctuary was the key which unlocked the mystery of the disappointment of 1844. It opened to view a complete system of truth, connected and harmonious, showing that God's hand had directed the great advent movement and revealing present duty as it brought to light the position and work of His people. As the disciples of Jesus after the terrible night of their anguish and disappointment were "glad when they saw the Lord," so did those now rejoice who had looked in faith for His second coming. They had expected Him to appear in glory to give reward to His servants. As their hopes were disappointed, they had lost sight of Jesus, and with Mary at the sepulcher they cried: "They have taken away my Lord, and I know not where they have laid Him." Now in the holy of holies they again beheld Him, their compassionate High Priest, soon to appear as their king and deliverer. Light from the sanctuary illumined the past, the present, and the future. They knew that God had led them by His unerring providence. Though, like the first disciples, they themselves had failed to understand the message which they bore, yet it had been in every respect correct. In proclaiming it they had fulfilled the purpose of God, and their labor had not been in vain in the Lord. Begotten "again unto a lively hope," they rejoiced "with joy unspeakable and full of glory."

Both the prophecy of Daniel 8:14, "Unto two thousand and three hundred days; then shall the sanctuary be cleansed," and the first angel's message, "Fear God, and give glory to Him; for the hour of His judgment is come," pointed to Christ's ministration in the most holy place, to the investigative judgment, and not to the coming of Christ for the redemption of His people and the destruction of the wicked. The mistake had not been in the reckoning of the prophetic periods, but in the *event* to take place at the end of the 2300 days. Through this error the believers had suffered disappointment, yet all that was foretold by the prophecy, and all that they had any Scripture warrant to expect, had been accomplished. At the very time when they were lamenting the failure of their hopes, the event had taken place which was foretold by the message, and which must be fulfilled before the Lord could appear to give reward to His servants.

Christ had come, not to the earth, as they expected, but, as fore-shadowed in the type, to the most holy place of the temple of God in heaven. He is represented by the prophet Daniel as coming at this time to the Ancient of Days: "I saw in the night visions, and, behold, one like the Son of man came with the clouds of heaven, and came"—not to the earth, but—"to the Ancient of Days, and they brought Him near before Him." Daniel 7:13.

This coming is foretold also by the prophet Malachi: "The Lord, whom ye seek, shall suddenly come to His temple, even the Messenger of the covenant, whom ye delight in: behold, He shall come, saith the Lord of hosts." Malachi 3:1. The coming of the Lord to His temple was sudden, unexpected, to His people. They were not looking to Him *there*. They expected Him to come to earth, "in flaming fire taking vengeance on them that know not God, and that obey not the gospel." 2 Thessalonians 1:8.

But the people were not yet ready to meet their Lord. There was still a work of preparation to be accomplished for them. Light was to be given, directing their minds to the temple of God in heaven; and as they should by faith follow their High Priest in His ministration there, new duties would be revealed. Another message of warning and instruction was to be given to the church.

Says the prophet: "Who may abide the day of His coming? and who shall stand when He appeareth? for He is like a refiner's fire, and like fullers' soap: and He shall sit as a refiner and purifier of silver: and He shall purify the sons of Levi, and purge them as gold and silver, that they may offer unto the Lord an offering in righteousness." Malachi 3:2, 3. Those who are living upon the earth when the intercession of Christ shall cease in the sanctuary above are to stand in the sight of a holy God without a mediator. Their robes must be spotless, their characters must be purified from sin by the blood of sprinkling. Through the grace of God and their own diligent effort they must be conquerors in the battle with evil. While the investigative judgment is going forward in heaven, while the sins of penitent believers are being removed from the sanctuary, there is to be a special work of purification, of putting away of sin, among God's people upon earth. This work is more clearly presented in the messages of Revelation 14.

When this work shall have been accomplished, the followers of Christ will be ready for His appearing. "Then shall the offering of Judah and Jerusalem be pleasant unto the Lord, as in the days of old, and as in former years." Malachi 3:4. Then the church which our Lord at His coming is to receive to Himself will be a "glorious church, not having spot, or wrinkle, or any such thing." Ephesians 5:27. Then she will look "forth as the morning, fair as the moon, clear as the sun, and terrible as an army with banners." Song of Solomon 6:10.

Besides the coming of the Lord to His temple, Malachi also foretells His second advent, His coming for the execution of the judgment, in these words: "And I will come near to you to judgment; and I will be a swift witness against the sorcerers, and against the adulterers, and against false swearers, and against those that oppress the hireling in his wages, the widow, and the fatherless, and that turn aside the stranger from his right, and fear not Me, saith the Lord of hosts." Malachi 3:5. Jude refers to the same scene when he says, "Behold, the Lord cometh with ten thousands of His saints, to execute judgment upon all, and to convince all that are ungodly among them of all their ungodly deeds." Jude 14, 15. This coming, and the coming of the Lord to His temple, are distinct and separate events.

The coming of Christ as our high priest to the most holy place, for the cleansing of the sanctuary, brought to view in Daniel 8:14; the coming of the Son of man to the Ancient of Days, as presented in Daniel 7:13; and the coming of the Lord to His temple, foretold by Malachi, are descriptions of the same event; and this is also represented by the coming of the bridegroom to the marriage, described by Christ in the parable of the ten virgins, of Matthew 25.

In the summer and autumn of 1844 the proclamation, "Behold, the Bridegroom cometh," was given. The two classes represented by the wise and foolish virgins were then developed—one class who looked with joy to the Lord's appearing, and who had been diligently preparing to meet Him; another class that, influenced by fear and acting from impulse, had been satisfied with a theory of the truth, but were destitute of the grace of God. In the parable, when the bridegroom came, "they that were ready went in with him to the marriage." The coming of the bridegroom, here brought to view, takes place before the marriage. The marriage represents the reception by Christ of His kingdom. The Holy City, the New Jerusalem, which is the capital and representative of the kingdom, is called "the bride, the Lamb's wife." Said the angel to John: "Come hither, I will show thee the bride, the Lamb's wife." "He carried me away in the spirit," says the prophet, "and showed me that great city, the holy Jerusalem, descending out of heaven from God." Revelation 21:9, 10. Clearly, then, the bride represents the Holy City, and the virgins that go out to meet the bridegroom are a symbol of the church. In the Revelation the people of God are said to be the guests at the marriage supper. Revelation 19:9. If *guests*, they cannot be represented also as the *bride*. Christ, as stated by the prophet Daniel, will receive from the Ancient of Days in heaven, "dominion, and glory, and a kingdom;" He will receive the New Jerusalem, the capital of His kingdom, "prepared as a bride adorned for her husband." Daniel 7:14; Revelation 21:2. Having received the kingdom, He will come in His glory, as King of kings and Lord of lords, for the redemption of His people, who are to "sit down with Abraham, and Isaac, and Jacob," at His table in His kingdom (Matthew 8:11; Luke 22:30), to partake of the marriage supper of the Lamb.

The proclamation, "Behold, the Bridegroom cometh," in the summer of 1844, led thousands to expect the immediate advent of the Lord. At the appointed time the Bridegroom came, not to the earth, as the people expected, but to the Ancient of Days in heaven, to the marriage, the reception of His kingdom. "They that were ready went in with Him to the marriage: and the door was shut." They were not to be present in person at the marriage; for it takes place in heaven, while they are upon the earth. The followers of Christ are to "wait for their Lord, when He will *return from* the wedding." Luke 12:36. But they are to understand His work, and to follow Him by faith as He goes in before God. It is in this sense that they are said to go in to the marriage.

In the parable it was those that had oil in their vessels with their lamps that went in to the marriage. Those who, with a knowledge of the truth from the Scriptures, had also the Spirit and grace of God, and who, in the night of their bitter trial, had patiently waited, searching the Bible for clearer light—these saw the truth concerning the sanctuary in heaven and the Saviour's change in ministration, and by faith they followed Him in His work in the sanctuary above. And all who through the testimony of the Scriptures accept the same truths, following Christ by faith as He enters in before God to perform the last work of mediation, and at its close to receive His kingdom—all these are represented as going in to the marriage.

In the parable of Matthew 22 the same figure of the marriage is introduced, and the investigative judgment is clearly represented as taking place before the marriage. Previous to the wedding the king comes in to see the guests, to see if all are attired in the wedding garment, the spotless robe of character washed and made white in the blood of the Lamb. Matthew 22:11; Revelation 7:14. He who is found wanting is cast out, but all who upon examination are seen to have the wedding garment on are accepted of God and accounted worthy of a share in His kingdom and a seat upon His throne. This work of examination of character, of determining who are prepared for the kingdom of God, is that of the investigative judgment, the closing work in the sanctuary above.

When the work of investigation shall be ended, when the cases of those who in all ages have professed to be followers of Christ have been examined and decided, then, and not till then, probation will close, and the door of mercy will be shut. Thus in the one short sentence, "They that were ready went in with Him to the marriage: and the door was shut," we are carried down through the Saviour's final ministration, to the time when the great work for man's salvation shall be completed.

In the service of the earthly sanctuary, which, as we have seen, is a figure of the service in the heavenly, when the high priest on the Day of Atonement entered the most holy place, the ministration in the first apartment ceased. God commanded: "There shall be no man in the tabernacle of the congregation when he goeth in to make an atonement in the holy place, until he comes out." Leviticus 16:17. So when Christ entered the holy of holies to perform the closing work of the atonement, He ceased His ministration in the first apartment. But when the ministration in the first apartment ended, the ministration in the second apartment began. When in the typical service the high priest left the holy on the Day of Atonement, he went in before God to present the blood of the sin offering in behalf of all Israel who truly repented of their sins. So Christ had only completed one part of His work as our intercessor, to enter upon another portion of the work, and He still pleaded His blood before the Father in behalf of sinners.

This subject was not understood by Adventists in 1844. After the passing of the time when the Saviour was expected, they still believed

His coming to be near; they held that they had reached an important crisis and that the work of Christ as man's intercessor before God had ceased. It appeared to them to be taught in the Bible that man's probation would close a short time before the actual coming of the Lord in the clouds of heaven. This seemed evident from those scriptures which point to a time when men will seek, knock, and cry at the door of mercy, and it will not be opened. And it was a question with them whether the date to which they had looked for the coming of Christ might not rather mark the beginning of this period which was immediately to precede His coming. Having given the warning of the judgment near, they felt that their work for the world was done, and they lost their burden of soul for the salvation of sinners, while the bold and blasphemous scoffing of the ungodly seemed to them another evidence that the Spirit of God had been withdrawn from the rejecters of His mercy. All this confirmed them in the belief that probation had ended, or, as they then expressed it, "the door of mercy was shut."

But clearer light came with the investigation of the sanctuary question. They now saw that they were correct in believing that the end of the 2300 days in 1844 marked an important crisis. But while it was true that that door of hope and mercy by which men had for eighteen hundred years found access to God, was closed, another door was opened, and forgiveness of sins was offered to men through the intercession of Christ in the most holy. One part of His ministration had closed, only to give place to another. There was still an "open door" to the heavenly sanctuary, where Christ was ministering in the sinner's behalf.

Now was seen the application of those words of Christ in the Revelation, addressed to the church at this very time: "These things saith He that is holy, He that is true, He that hath the key of David, He that openeth, and no man shutteth; and shutteth, and no man openeth; I know thy works: behold, I have set before thee an open door, and no man can shut it." Revelation 3:7, 8.

It is those who by faith follow Jesus in the great work of the atonement who receive the benefits of His mediation in their behalf, while those who reject the light which brings to view this work of ministration are not benefited thereby. The Jews who rejected the light given at Christ's first advent, and refused to believe on Him as the Saviour of the world, could not receive pardon through Him. When Jesus at His ascension entered by His own blood into the heavenly sanctuary to shed upon His disciples the blessings of His mediation, the Jews were left in total darkness to continue their useless sacrifices and offerings. The ministration of types and shadows had ceased. That door by which men had formerly found access to God was no longer open. The Jews had refused to seek Him in the only way whereby He could then be found, through the ministration in the sanctuary in heaven. Therefore they found no communion with God. To them the door was shut. They had no knowledge of Christ as the true sacrifice and the only mediator before God; hence they could not receive the benefits of His mediation.

The condition of the unbelieving Jews illustrates the condition of the careless and unbelieving among professed Christians, who are willingly ignorant of the work of our merciful High Priest. In the typical service, when the high priest entered the most holy place, all Israel were required to gather about the sanctuary and in the most solemn manner humble their souls before God, that they might receive the pardon of their sins and not be cut off from the congregation. How much more essential in this antitypical Day of Atonement that we understand the work of our High Priest and know what duties are required of us.

Men cannot with impunity reject the warning which God in mercy sends them. A message was sent from heaven to the world in Noah's day, and their salvation depended upon the manner in which they treated that message. Because they rejected the warning, the Spirit of God was withdrawn from the sinful race, and they perished in the waters of the Flood. In the time of Abraham, mercy ceased to plead with the guilty inhabitants of Sodom, and all but Lot with his wife and two daughters were consumed by the fire sent down from heaven. So in the days of Christ. The Son of God declared to the unbelieving Jews of that generation: "Your house is left unto you desolate." Matthew 23:38. Looking down to the last days, the same Infinite Power declares, concerning those who "received not the love of the truth, that they might be saved": "For this cause God shall send them strong delusion, that they should believe a lie: that they all might be damned who believed not the truth, but had pleasure in unrighteousness." 2 Thessalonians 2:10-12. As they reject the teachings of His word, God withdraws His Spirit and leaves them to the deceptions which they love.

But Christ still intercedes in man's behalf, and light will be given to those who seek it. Though this was not at first understood by Adventists, it was afterward made plain as the Scriptures which define their true position began to open before them.

The passing of the time in 1844 was followed by a period of great trial to those who still held the advent faith. Their only relief, so far as ascertaining their true position was concerned, was the light which directed their minds to the sanctuary above. Some renounced their faith in their former reckoning of the prophetic periods and ascribed to human or satanic agencies the powerful influence of the Holy Spirit which had attended the advent movement. Another class firmly held that the Lord had led them in their past experience; and as they waited and watched and prayed to know the will of God they saw that their great High Priest had entered upon another work of ministration, and, following Him by faith, they were led to see also the closing work of the church. They had a clearer understanding of the first and second angels' messages, and were prepared to receive and give to the world the solemn warning of the third angel of Revelation 14.

omplete Your Set!

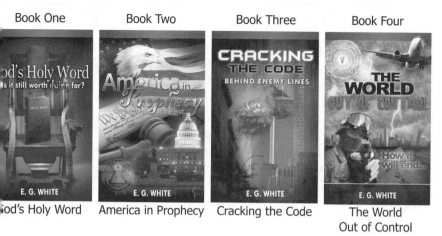

Book One	Book Two	Book Three	Book Four
od's Holy Word	America in Prophecy	Cracking the Code	The World Out of Control

the world buckles under the weight of catastrophe—9/11, the great tsunami, rthquakes, forest fires, and wave after wave of hurricanes—this book reveals that ese are but a fraction of the destructive forces that are yet to come. With so many ses—the ongoing war on terror; an increase in brutal crimes, especially against ldren; economic and political instability; lawlessness and confusion; and the oliferation and acceptance of immorality—mainstream, secular media outlets are king, "Is this the end of the world?"

e key to answering this question is looking into a long-forgotten past. In this classic sterpiece by one of the world's most influential writers, you'll begin to understand the aclysmic events battering our world in a new light. You'll see how and why history eats itself, yet more dangerously than in previous times.

different than anything you've ever read, but authenticated by hundreds of Bible ses and keen insight, This set is an eye-opening journey through human history and ond that plunges you headfirst into the ultimate battle between good and evil.

ecial Edition Complete Series

s special edition book contains all four books of the series der one cover. This must-read masterpiece has given owledge and assurance to millions. Now it's your turn to e the answers you need to face the future.

Now 1-800-423-1319 or visit www.RemnantPublications.com

ARE YOU SEARCHING FOR TRUTH?

Do you need reliable answers to urgent questions?

- *Can we know and understand the future?*
- *What are the tests of a true prophet?*
- *Is the development of character important?*
- *Are there physical and spiritual laws for health and happiness?*
- *What really happens to us after death?*
- *Is it possible to live forever?*
- *How can you find inner peace in a world of chaos?*

Discover the answers to these and other vital questions by enrolling in our Bible Correspondence Course. We care about you and your welfare. Thats why we prepared this series of thought-provoking Bible study lessons to help people just like you. These lessons will stimulate you to think independently, and help you conscientiously make the choices which will make you happy.

The first two lessons in the series are free of charge. If you like the lessons, we ask you to include a nominal freewill offering, beginning with lesson three, to help cover postage and handling.

Do You Want To Know More?

Yes, Please send me, at no charge, the first two lessons.

Name _____

Address_____

City_____ State _____

Zip_____

Send to:

**Bible Correspondence Course
P.O. Box 426
Coldwater, MI 49036**

GC4 08